The Complete Book of Time & Money

Grades K-3

Thinking Kids®
Carson-Dellosa Publishing LLC
Greensboro, North Carolina

Thinking Kids®
Carson-Dellosa Publishing LLC
PO Box 35665
Greensboro, NC 27425 USA

ISBN 978-1-4838-2691-2

Table of Contents

Time to the Quarter-Hour

Time to the Minute

Time Review

Coins and Bills

Review

Name_____

Face Clocks: Introduction

What is the best way to tell what time it is? **A clock!**

There are all kinds of clocks. **Circle** the ones you have seen.

Face Clocks: Identifying Parts

A clock has different parts.

Read and **trace** each part of the clock.

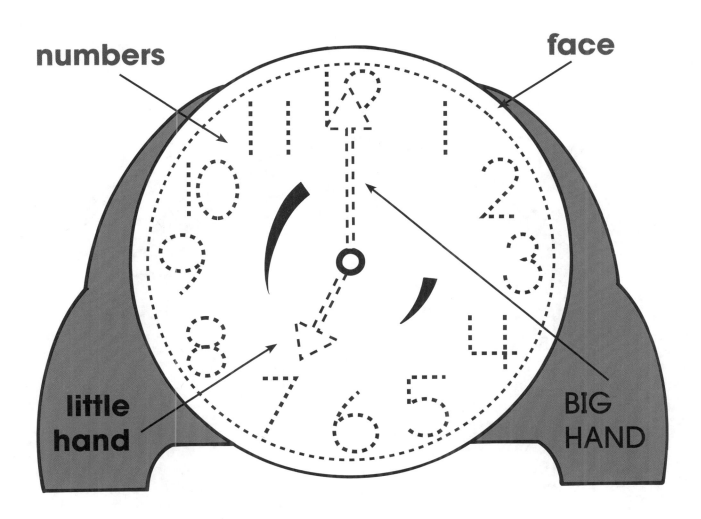

numbers

face

little hand

BIG HAND

The BIG HAND is on **12**.
The **little hand** tells the hour.

Face Clocks: Identifying Parts

A clock face has numbers.

Trace the numbers on the clock.

Writing the Time

Learning to tell time is fun! A clock tells us the time.

Write the numbers on the clock face.
Draw the BIG HAND to **12**.
Draw the **little hand** to **5**.

It is 5 o'clock.

Writing the Time

An **hour** is **60 minutes** long.

It takes an **hour** for the BIG HAND to go around the clock.

When the BIG HAND is on **12** and the **little hand** points to a number, that number is **the hour!**

The BIG HAND is on the **12**. **Color** it red.

The **little hand** is on the **8**. **Color** it blue.

The BIG HAND is on _____.

The **little hand** is on _____.

It is _____ o'clock.

Name_____

Writing the Time

Color each **little hour hand** blue.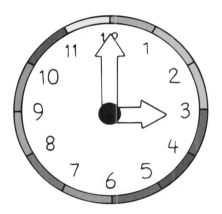

Fill in the blanks.

The BIG HAND is on _____.

The **little hand** is on _____.

It is _____ o'clock.

The BIG HAND is on _____.

The **little hand** is on _____.

It is _____ o'clock.

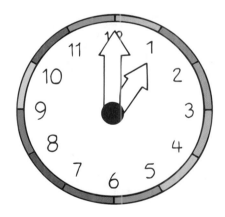

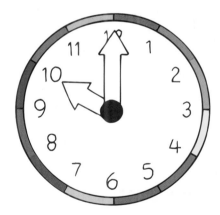

The BIG HAND is on _____.

The **little hand** is on _____.

It is _____ o'clock.

The BIG HAND is on _____.

The **little hand** is on _____.

It is _____ o'clock.

Name_____

Writing the Time

Color each **little hour hand** blue.

Fill in the blanks.

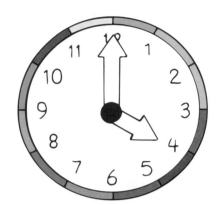

The BIG HAND is on _____.

The **little hand** is on _____.

It is _____ o'clock.

The BIG HAND is on _____.

The **little hand** is on _____.

It is _____ o'clock.

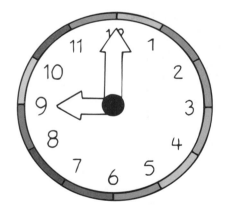

The BIG HAND is on _____.

The **little hand** is on _____.

It is _____ o'clock.

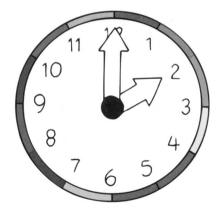

The BIG HAND is on _____.

The **little hand** is on _____.

It is _____ o'clock.

Drawing the Hour Hand

If the BIG HAND is on **12**, it is easy to tell the time.

Look at the little hand to see the hour.

Trace the **little hand** to make the hour **10 o'clock.**

The BIG HAND is on _____.

The **little hand** is on _____.

It is _____ o'clock.

Drawing the Hour Hand

Draw the **little hour hand** on each clock.

8 o'clock

1 o'clock

7 o'clock

Drawing the Hour Hand

Draw the **little hour hand** on each clock.

4 o'clock

11 o'clock

5 o'clock

Name_____

Drawing the Hour Hand

Draw the **little hour hand** on each clock.

2 o'clock

10 o'clock

9 o'clock

Name_____

Drawing the Hour Hand

Draw the **little hour hand** on each clock.

6 o'clock

12 o'clock

3 o'clock

Circling the Hour Hand

Circle the **little hour hand** on each clock.

What time is it? Write the time below.

_____ o'clock

_____ o'clock

_____ o'clock

_____ o'clock

_____ o'clock

_____ o'clock

Name_____

Circling the Hour Hand

Circle the **little hour hand** on each clock.

What time is it? Write the time below.

_____ o'clock

_____ o'clock

_____ o'clock

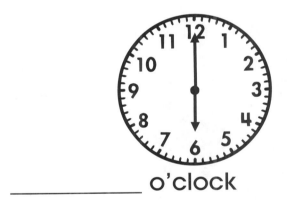

_____ o'clock

_____ o'clock

_____ o'clock

Practice

Here's the scoop!

Draw the **little hour hand** on each clock.

8 o'clock   4 o'clock   2 o'clock

6 o'clock   11 o'clock   3 o'clock

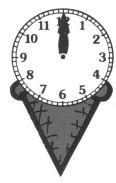

1 o'clock   5 o'clock   7 o'clock

Practice

What time is it?

Write the time below each clock.

_____ o'clock

_____ o'clock

_____ o'clock

_____ o'clock

_____ o'clock

_____ o'clock

Practice

What is the time?

Write the time below each clock.

_____ o'clock

_____ o'clock

_____ o'clock

_____ o'clock

_____ o'clock

_____ o'clock

Practice

What is the time?

Write the time below each clock.

____ o'clock   ____ o'clock   ____ o'clock

____ o'clock   ____ o'clock   ____ o'clock

____ o'clock   ____ o'clock   ____ o'clock

____ o'clock   ____ o'clock

Practice

What is the time? It's Clown Time!

Write the time below each clock.

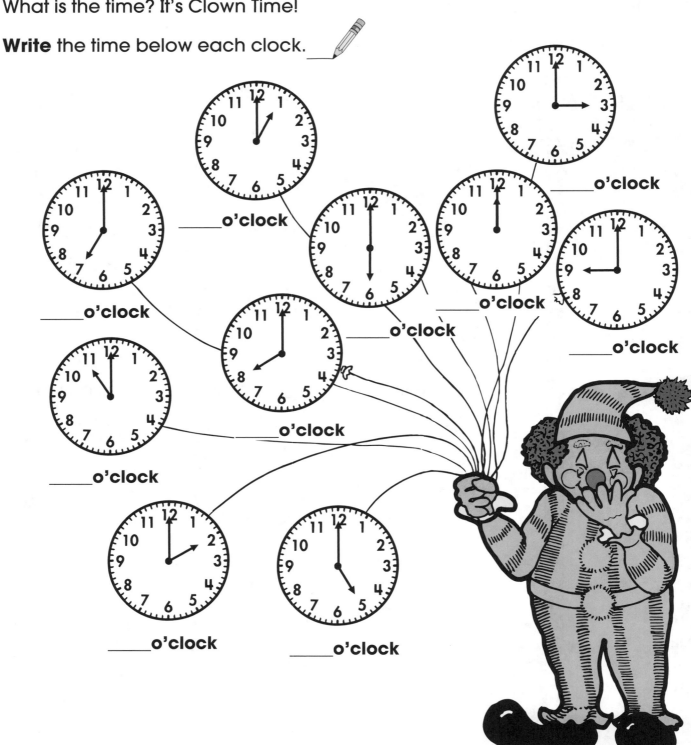

_____ o'clock

_____ o'clock

_____ o'clock

_____ o'clock

_____ o'clock

_____ o'clock

_____ o'clock

_____ o'clock

_____ o'clock

_____ o'clock

_____ o'clock

Name_____

Writing the Time: One Hour Later

When I go to my friend's house to play, Mom says to come home **one hour later**.

Write the original time and **one hour later**.

Writing the Time: One Hour Later

Draw the **little hands** on the clocks to show **one hour later**.

Write the times.

_____   _____

_____   _____

_____   _____

Name_____

Writing the Time: One Hour Later

Draw the **little hands** on the clocks to show **one hour later**.

Write the times.

_____

_____

_____

Writing the Time: One Hour Later

Draw the **little hands** on the clocks to show **one hour later**.

Write the times.

Time Poems

Read each poem.

Draw a line to the clock that matches.

A. It is 7 o'clock.
   Time to rise and shine.
   First it will rain,
   Then turn out fine.

B. It is 4 o'clock.
   It is time to play!
   We will see friends
   Outside today.

C. It is 10 o'clock.
   We are at the pool.
   We're happy today
   Because there is no school!

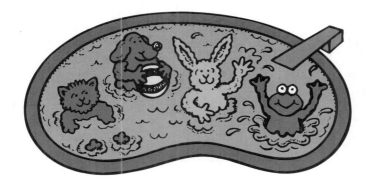

Name_____

Time Poems

Read each poem.

Draw a line to the clock that matches.

A. It is 2 o'clock.
   Now it is night.
   I am in bed,
   All tucked in tight.

B. It is 12 o'clock,
   And time to eat.
   Have a sandwich,
   Then a treat!

C. It is 5 o'clock.
   Night is almost here.
   Evening shadows
   Are very near.

Time Poems

Read each poem.

Draw a line to the clock that matches.

A. It is 8 o'clock.
   Now dinner is done.
   Time for homework
   And then some fun.

B. It is 11 o'clock,
   And I am in bed
   With a pillow
   Underneath my head.

C. It is 3 o'clock.
   We are out the door
   To run and play,
   Then play some more.

Digital Clocks: Introduction

This is a **digital clock**.

It tells time with **numbers**.

First, it tells the **hour**, then the **minutes**.

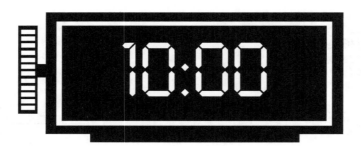

 Draw the **little hour hand** on this face clock to make it read **10 o'clock**.

Now, both clocks show that it is **10 o'clock**.

 Draw a **green circle** around each kind of clock you have at home.

Matching Digital and Face Clocks

Trace the time on the **digital clocks**.

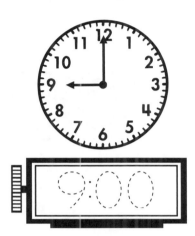

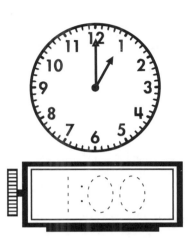

Match each face clock with the correct digital clock.

Matching Digital and Face Clocks

Match each digital clock with the correct face clock.

Matching Digital and Face Clocks

Match the digital and face clocks.

Matching Digital and Face Clocks

Match the digital and face clocks.

Name_____

Digital Clocks

Write the time on the digital clocks.

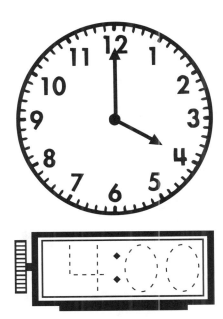

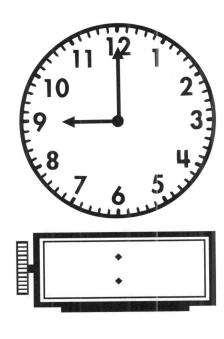

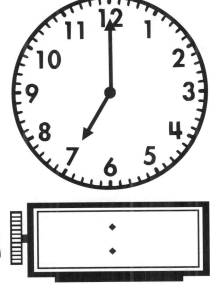

Name_____

Digital Clocks

Write the time on the digital clocks.

Digital Clocks

Write the time on the digital clocks.

Name_____

Drawing the Hour Hand:
Matching Digital and Face Clocks

Look at each digital clock. **Say** the time.

Draw the **little hour hand** on each face clock.

Name_____

Drawing the Hour Hand: Matching Digital and Face Clocks

Look at each digital clock. **Say** the time.

Draw the **little hour hand** on each face clock.

Drawing the Hour Hand: Matching Digital and Face Clocks

Look at each digital clock. **Say** the time.

Draw the **little hour hand** on each face clock.

Name_____

Time Two Ways

Show each time **two ways**. **Draw** the hands on each face clock.

Write the time on each digital clock.

A. Bessie Bear wakes up at **6 o'clock**.

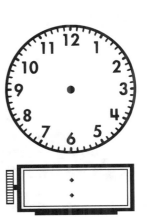

B. Bernie Bear eats breakfast at **7 o'clock**.

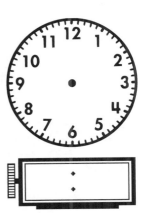

C. What time do you wake up on school mornings?
Draw yourself waking up.

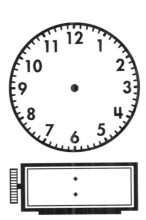

Time Two Ways

Show each time **two ways**. **Draw** the hands on each face clock.

Write the time on each digital clock.

A.   Randy Rabbit leaves for school at **8 o'clock**.

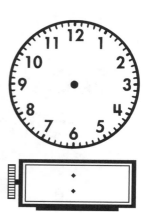

B.   Rebecca Rabbit goes out to recess at **10 o'clock**.

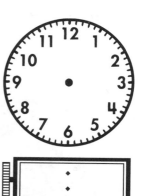

C.   What time do you go out for recess?
     Draw yourself at recess.

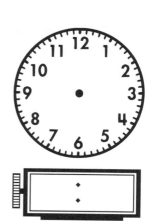

Name_____

Time Two Ways

Show each time **two ways**. **Draw** the hands on each face clock.

Write the time on each digital clock.

A.   Fernando Frog eats lunch at **12 o'clock**.

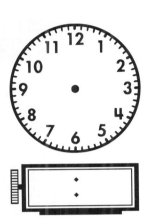

B.   Fanny Frog goes to the library at **1 o'clock**.

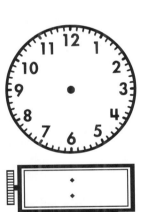

C.   What time do you eat lunch?
     Draw yourself eating lunch.

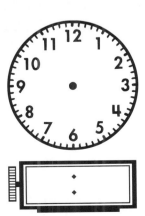

Time Two Ways

Show each time **two ways**. **Draw** the hands on each face clock.

Write the time on each digital clock.

A.   At **9 o'clock,** Freddie Frog goes for a swim.

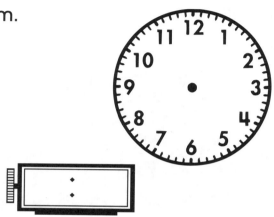

B.   At **11 o'clock,** Freddie Frog sits on a lily pad.
     Draw a picture.

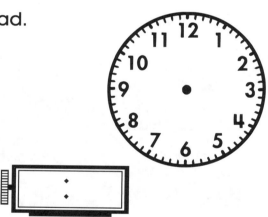

C.   At **3 o'clock,** Freddie Frog eats a snack.
     Draw a picture.

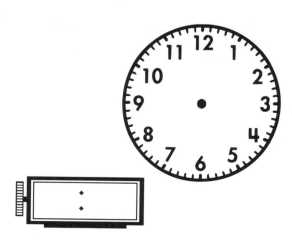

Time Stories

Read each story. **Draw** the hands on each face clock.

A. At **11:00**, Mouse
    starts to cook.
    Yum! Cheese
    soup is good.

B. At **12 o'clock**,
    Mouse sets the
    table. Uh-oh! He
    drops a spoon.

C. At **7:00**, Mouse
    reads a book.
    What a funny story!

D. Time for bed. It is
    9 o'clock, and
    Mouse is sleepy.

Time Stories

Read each story. **Draw** the hands on each face clock.

A. Rabbit is hungry. It is **6 o'clock**—time for supper and some carrot stew.

B. At **8 o'clock**, Rabbit washes the dishes. Scrub, scrub! The pot is sticky.

C. Rabbit works in his garden. It is **4 o'clock**, and he is picking lettuce.

D. At **5:00**, Rabbit makes a lettuce salad. What a tasty meal!

Name_____

Time to the Half-Hour: Introduction

This clock face shows the time that has gone by since 8 o'clock.

Thirty minutes or **half an hour** has gone by.

There are three ways to say time to the half-hour.

We say **eight thirty, thirty past eight,** or **half past eight**.

Trace the original time and a half-hour later.

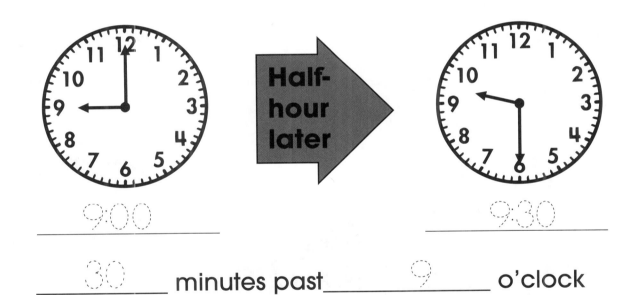

_____9:00_____   _____9:30_____

_____30_____ minutes past_____9_____ o'clock

Name_____

Writing Time on the Half-Hour

Draw the hands on each clock to show a **half-hour later**. **Write** each time.

Half-
hour
later

_____

_____ minutes past

_____ o'clock

Half-
hour
later

_____

_____ minutes past

_____ o'clock

Writing Time on the Half-Hour

What time is it?

half past_____

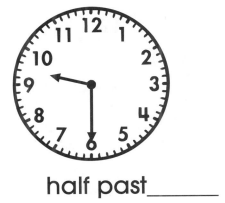

half past_____

half past_____

half past_____

half past_____

half past_____

Name_____

Writing Time on the Half-Hour

What time is it?

half past_____

half past_____

half past_____

half past_____

half past_____

half past_____

Name_____

Writing Time on the Half-Hour

Trace each BIG MINUTE HAND **green**.

Trace each **little hour hand** yellow.

Write the time on the line.

_____

_____

_____

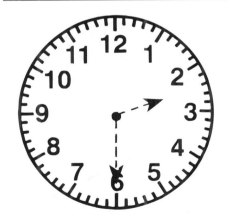

_____

Name_____

Writing Time on the Half-Hour

Trace each BIG MINUTE HAND **green**.

Trace each **little hour hand** yellow.

Write the time on the line.

_____

_____

Name_____

Writing Time on the Half-Hour

Who "nose" these times?

Write the time under each clock.

Color the noses.

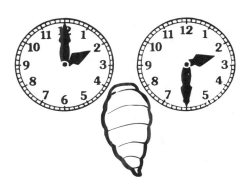

_____   _____   _____

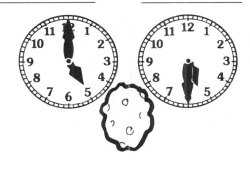

_____   _____   _____

_____   _____   _____

Writing Time on the Half-Hour

Who "nose" these times?

Write the time under each clock.

Color the noses.

_____   _____   _____   _____

_____   _____   _____   _____

_____   _____   _____   _____

Name_____

Matching Digital and Face Clocks

These digital clocks lost their numbers! Write each time next to its matching face clock on this page and pages 60-61.

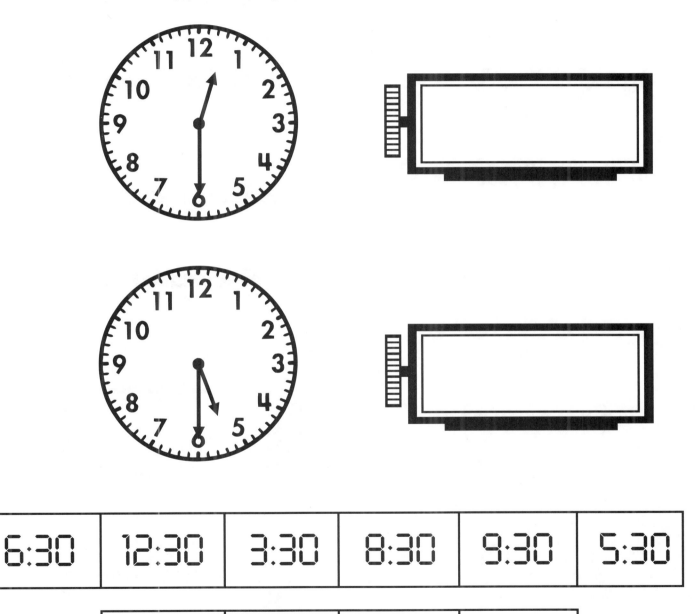

6:30	12:30	3:30	8:30	9:30	5:30

1:00	4:00	7:00	2:00

Matching Digital and Face Clocks

Matching Digital and Face Clocks

Name_____

Drawing the Hour Hand

Say the time. **Draw** the **little hour hand** on each clock.

Drawing the Hour Hand

Say the time. **Draw** the **little hour hand** on each clock.

Drawing the Hour Hand

Say the time. **Draw** the **little hour hand** on each clock.

Telling Time: Hour and Half-Hour

Draw a line from the clock to the correct time.

3:00

3:30

4:00

6:30

7:00

7:30

4:00

5:00

6:00

Name_____

Telling Time: Hour and Half-Hour

Draw a line from the clock to the correct time.

3:00

3:30

4:30

6:30

7:00

7:30

11:00

11:30

12:00

Name_____

Telling Time: Hour and Half-Hour

Draw a line from the clock to the correct time.

8:00

4:30

5:00

12:00

10:30

1:00

9:30

10:30

10:00

Name_____

Telling Time: Hour and Half-Hour

Draw a line from the clock to the correct time.

9:30

9:00

11:00

2:00

10:30

1:00

12:30

10:30

12:00

Name_____

Writing the Time: Practice

What time is it? It's space time! **Write** the time below each clock.

Name_____

Writing the Time: Practice

What time is it? It's space time! **Write** the time below each clock.

Writing the Time: Practice

Draw the hands on the sock clocks.

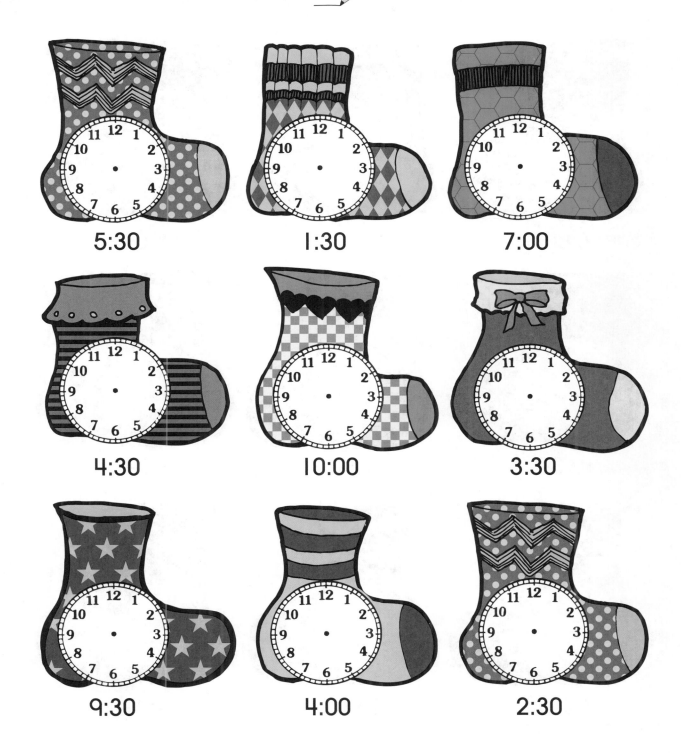

5:30

1:30

7:00

4:30

10:00

3:30

9:30

4:00

2:30

Writing the Time: Practice

Draw the hands on the sock clocks. _____

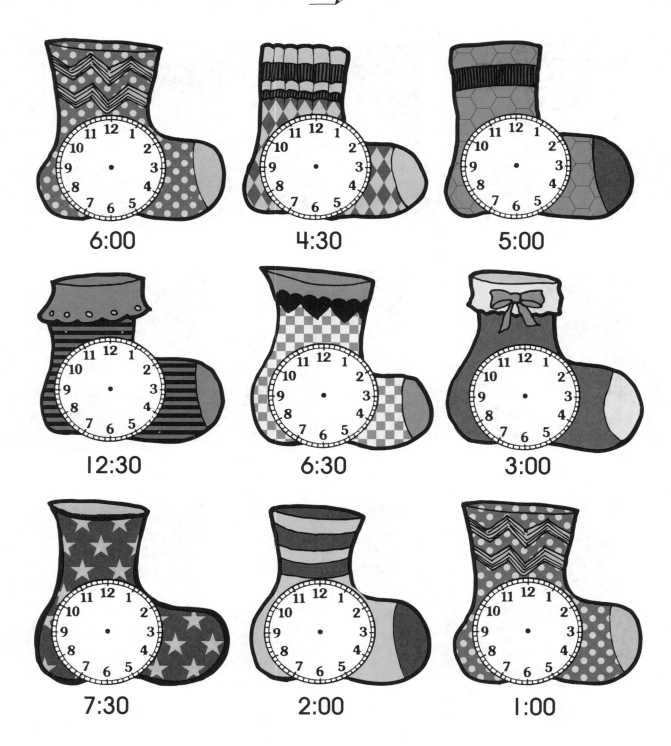

6:00   4:30   5:00

12:30   6:30   3:00

7:30   2:00   1:00

Name_____

Writing the Time: Practice

What time is it? **Write** the time below each clock.

:_____

:_____

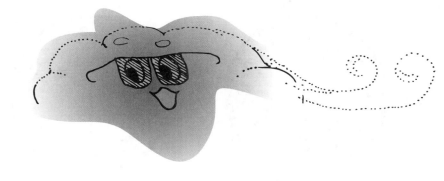

:_____

:_____

:_____

:_____

Name_____

Writing the Time: Practice

What time is it? **Write** the time below each clock.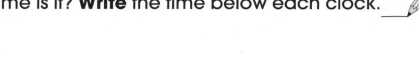

3:00
_____

_____:_____

_____:_____

_____:_____

_____:_____

_____:_____

Matching Digital and Face Clocks

Match each clock to the correct time.

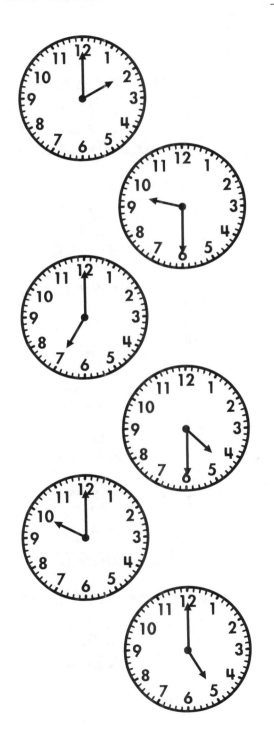

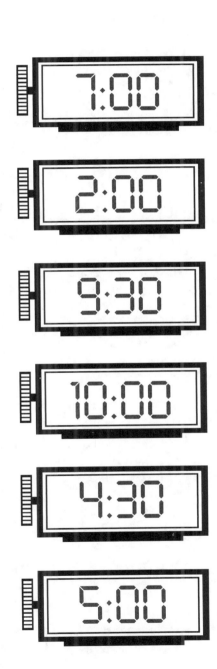

Matching Digital and Face Clocks

Match each clock to the correct time.

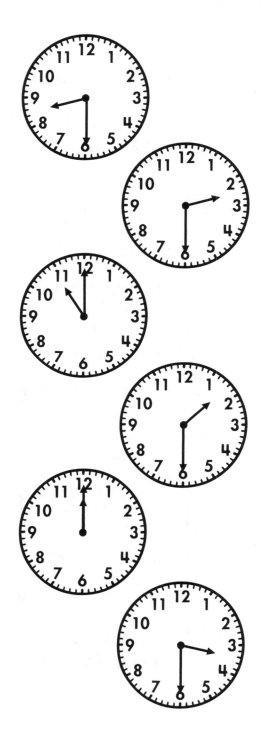

Name_____

Time Stories

Read each story. **Draw** the hands on each face clock.

A. Hop, hop! It is **10:30**, and Frog is going to the market.

B. At **11:30**, Frog heads home. She has a basket of tasty treats.

C. At **4:30**, Frog is making a cake. The little frogs will eat it.

D. By **7:30**, Frog's cake is all gone. My, that was good!

Name_____

Time Stories

Read each story. **Draw** the hands on each face clock.

A. It is **5:30**, and the sun is coming up. Bird is ready for the day.

B. At **6:30**, Bird is looking for breakfast. Watch out, worms!

C. Bird is resting after breakfast. It is **9:30**, and almost time for flying practice.

D. At **12:30**, Bird naps before lunch. Flying is hard work.

x

Time Lapse: Hours

Can you tell how much time has passed? **Write** the time below each clock.

Fill in the blanks.

__ : _____   __ : _____

It started snowing at **3:00** and snowed until **6:00**.

It snowed for _____ hours.

  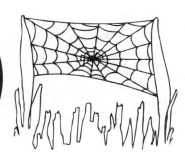

__ : _____   __ : _____

What time did the spider start spinning the web? ____ : _____

What time did she finish? ____ : _____

The spider took _____ hours to spin the web.

Name_____

Time Lapse: Hours

Can you tell how much time has passed? **Write** the time below each clock.

Fill in the blanks.

_____:_____   _____:_____

Dad went to the grocery store. Dad took _____ hour to buy groceries.

_____:_____   _____:_____

The teacher taught math class.

Math lasted _____ hour.

Time Lapse: Hours

It is important to get home when your parents expect you!

Steve went to play baseball at **3:30**. Mom told him to be home in **two hours**.

He should be home at _____ : _____ .

Show the time on this watch. _____

Tiffany went to Latonia's house to ride bikes at **10:00**. Dad asked her to be home in **three hours**.

She should be home at _____ : _____.

Show the time on this watch. _____

Time Lapse: Hours

Kristen took her sister to the movies at **7:30**. Mom said she would meet them in **two hours**.

She will meet them at _____ : _____.

Show the time on this watch.

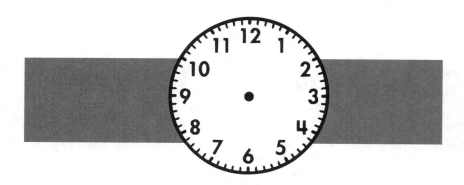

Latrissa went to the library for story hour. She got there at **1:00**. She stayed **one hour**.

Story hour should be over at _____ : _____ .

Show the time Latrissa left for home.

Name_____

Drawing the Hour Hand:
A Half-Hour Later

Trace and draw the hands on each face clock.

A. At **7:00**, Bill turns the TV on.

What time is it one half-hour later?

B. At **4:00**, we all jump in the car.

What time is it one half-hour later?

Name_____

Drawing the Hour Hand:
A Half-Hour Later

Draw the hands on each face clock.

A. At **8:00**, it starts to rain.

What time is it one half-hour later?

B. At **11:00**, the sun comes out.

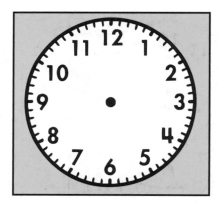

What time is it one half-hour later?

Name_____

Drawing the Hour Hand:
A Half-Hour Later

Draw the hands on each face clock.

A. At **6:30**, a fire engine roars down the street.

What time is it one half-hour later?

B. At **11:30**, everyone is playing in the schoolyard.

What time is it one half-hour later?

C. At **5:30**, my dog gets out of the yard.

What time is it one half-hour later?

Time Stories

Read each story. **Draw** the hands on each face clock.

A. Tom makes a huge sandwich at **1:00**. He finishes the whole sandwich **one half-hour** later. What time does Tom finish the sandwich?

B. Tom gets home from school at **3:00**. He goes out to play **30 minutes** later. What time does Tom go out to play?

C. Tom goes to bed at **8:30**. He falls asleep **one half-hour** later. What time does Tom fall asleep?

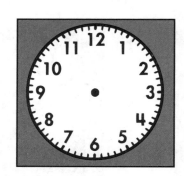

Time Stories

Read each story. **Draw** the hands on each face clock.

A. Maria walks to the bus stop at **7:00**. She gets on the bus **30 minutes** later. What time does she get on the bus?

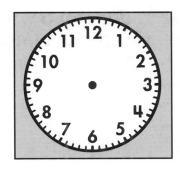

B. Maria helps make dinner at **5:30**. Everyone eats **one half-hour** later. What time does everyone eat?

C. Maria's family plays a game at **8:00**. They stop playing **30 minutes** later. What time do they stop playing?

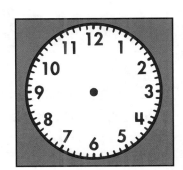

Name_____

Time Stories

Read each story. **Draw** the hands on each face clock.

A. Li goes for a walk at **10:30**. He comes back with three friends **30 minutes** later. What time does he come back with his friends?

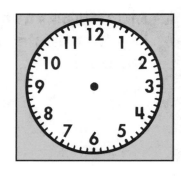

B. Li gets on his bike at **3:30**. He reaches the library **one half-hour** later. What time does he reach the library?

C. Li heads home at **5:00**. He gets home **30 minutes** later. What time does he get home?

Name_____

Time Two Ways

Draw the hands on each face clock. **Write** the time on each digital clock.

A. At **1:30**, Squirrel hides seven nuts.

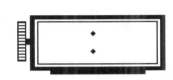

B. At **2:00**, Squirrel runs down the tree to find more nuts.

C. By **3:30**, Squirrel is ready for a long rest.

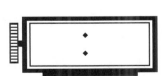

Name_____

Time Two Ways

Draw the hands on each face clock. **Write** the time on each digital clock.

A. At **5:30**, Toad hops over to visit Frog.

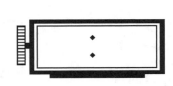

B. At **6:00**, Frog and Toad are sipping Fine Fly Tea.

C. By **7:30**, Toad heads home, full of tea and bug cakes.

Time Two Ways

Draw the hands on each face clock. **Write** the time on each digital clock.

A. Maria Mouse reaches the library at **11 o'clock**. She leaves the library at **11:30**.

Reaches library   Leaves the library

B. Marcus Mouse reaches Pizza Palace at **3 o'clock**. He finishes his pizza at **3:30**.

Reaches Pizza Palace   Finishes pizza

Time Two Ways

Draw the hands on each face clock. **Write** the time on each digital clock.

A. Tim Toad begins planting the garden at **9 o'clock**. He finishes planting at **11:30**.

Begins planting   **Finishes planting**

B. Tara Toad starts roller-skating at **10 o'clock**. She stops roller-skating **30 minutes after 10 o'clock**.

Starts roller-skating   **Stops roller-skating**

Time Two Ways

Draw the hands on each face clock. **Write** the time on each digital clock.

A. Ricardo Raccoon starts eating his lunch at **12:00**. He finishes his lunch **30 minutes after 12:00**.

Starts lunch　　　　　　　　　　　　Finishes lunch

B. Rachel Raccoon sits at the computer at **7:00**. She gets up a **half-hour after 7:00**.

Sits down　　　　　　　　　　　　　　Gets up

Time Stories

Read the story. **Write** the time two ways.

Bear is going on a picnic today with his brother and sister. They leave for the park at **9:00**. They get to the park at **10:00**. Bear helps carry the food to a picnic table. Then, he gets out his kite. Bear flies his kite at **10:30**. Later, at **11:30**, everyone has a picnic lunch!

Put the story in order by writing what time Bear does each thing.

Leaves for the park

Gets to the park

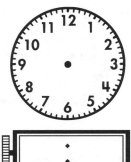

Flies kite

Eats lunch

Name_____

Time Stories

Read the story. **Write** the time two ways. ✏

Pig wakes up at **7:00**. Pig's grandmother is taking her to the zoo today! They get to the zoo at **10:30**. They walk and walk. They stop to eat at **12:30**. They walk some more. Pig and her grandmother don't get home until **5:30**. They had a wonderful day!

Put the story in order by writing what time Pig does each thing.

A. _____

B. _____

C. _____

D. _____

Name_____

Time Stories

Read the story. **Write** the time two ways.

It's a hot summer day. Frog and Turtle begin to walk to the lake at **11:00**. They jump into the cold water at **12:30**. They swim and dive. Then, they enjoy lunch at **1:30**. They fall asleep after lunch. Later, at **3:00**, Frog and Turtle wake up. They hurry home!

Put the story in order by writing what time Frog and Turtle do each thing.

A. _____   **B.** _____

C. _____   **D.** _____

Name_____

Time Puzzles

Read each "time clue." **Draw** the hands on each face clock.

Write the time on each digital clock.

A. It's dark outside.
    Everyone is asleep.

B. Ring, ring!
    Time to get up.

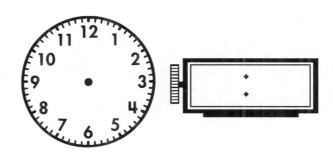

C. Here comes the school bus.
    Run, so you won't be late!

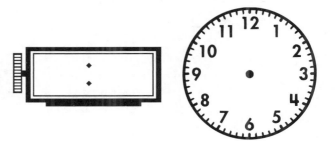

Name_____

Time Puzzles

Read each "time clue." **Draw** the hands on each face clock.

Write the time on each digital clock.

A.   I'm hungry! Soon it will
     be time for lunch.

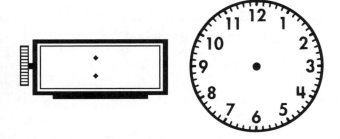

B.   School is out!
     We're going home.

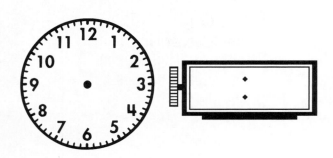

C.   Here comes the mail!
     I hope I get a letter.

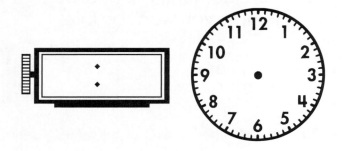

Time Puzzles

Read each "time clue." **Draw** the hands on each face clock.

Write the time on each digital clock.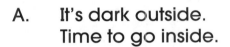

A. It's dark outside.
    Time to go inside.

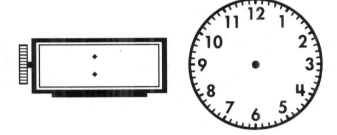

B. It's light tonight.
    Look, a big full moon!

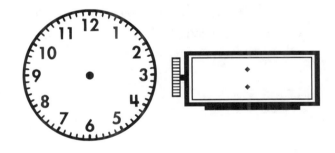

C. Sometimes I have
    homework to do.

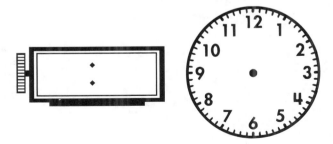

Time Puzzles

Read each "time clue." **Draw** the hands on each face clock.

Write the time on each digital clock.

A. Sometimes I have
    jobs to do.

B. The best time is when I can
    do just what I want to do.

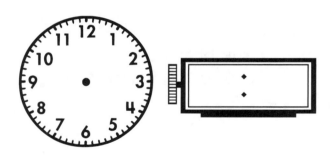

C. On Saturday and Sunday,
    I play with friends.

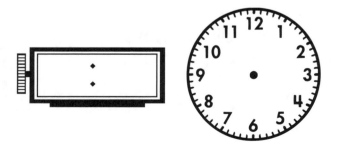

Name_____

Time to the Quarter-Hour: Introduction

Each **hour** has **60** minutes. An **hour** has **4 quarter-hours**. A **quarter-hour** is **15 minutes**.

This clock face shows a quarter-hour.

From the **12** to the **3** is **15 minutes**.

From the 12 to the 3 is 15 minutes.

_____**15**_____ minutes after _____**3**_____ o'clock

is _____**3:15**_____

Telling Time

Each **hour** has **4 quarter-hours**. A **quarter-hour** is **15 minutes**.

Write the original time and a quarter-hour later.

One quarter-hour later

_____ 9:00 _____   _____ 9:15 _____

_____ minutes past _____ 9 _____ o'clock

One quarter-Hour later

_____   _____

_____ minutes past _____ o'clock

Name_____

Telling Time

Draw the hands. Write the times.

5:15

___15___ minutes after
___5___ o'clock

10:15

_____ minutes after
_____ o'clock

2:15

_____ minutes after
_____ o'clock

9:15

_____ minutes after
_____ o'clock

Name_____

Telling Time

Draw the hands. Write the times.

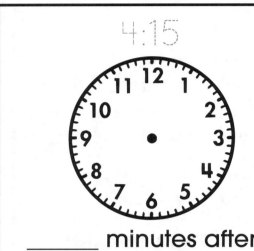

4:15

_____ minutes after

_____ o'clock

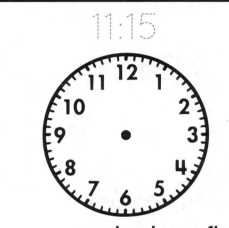

11:15

_____ minutes after

_____ o'clock

3:15

_____ minutes after

_____ o'clock

6:15

_____ minutes after

_____ o'clock

Name_____

Digital Clocks

Your **digital clock** has quarter-hours, too! It shows **15 minutes**. Write 15 minutes after each time.

 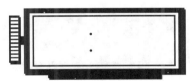

 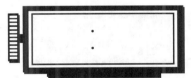

 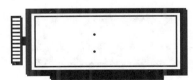

Name_____

Digital Clocks

Write 15 minutes after each time.

 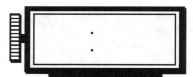

 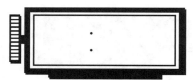

 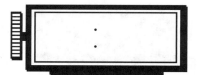

 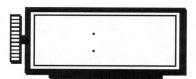

Name_____

Digital Clocks

Circle the correct digital time.

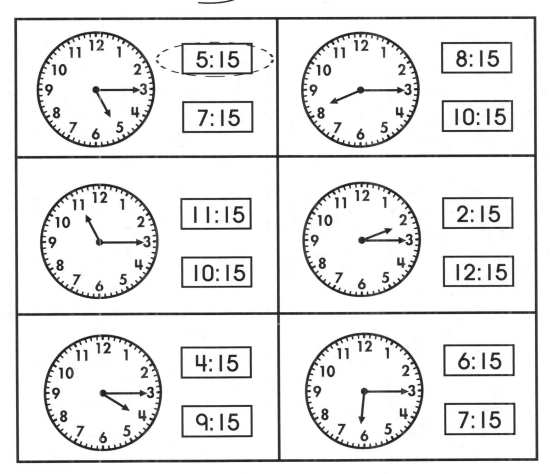

15 minutes past 6 is dinner time.

Draw the minute hand with an orange crayon.

Draw the hour hand with a **purple** crayon.

_____ minutes after _____ o'clock

6:15

Digital Clocks

Circle the correct digital time.

Clock	Options
	3:15 / 7:15
	8:15 / 7:15
	11:15 / 7:15
	2:15 / 1:15
	4:15 / 9:15
	10:15 / 7:15

15 minutes past 7 is when school starts.

Draw the minute hand with an orange crayon.

Draw the hour hand with a purple crayon.

_____ minutes after _____ o'clock

7:15

Telling Time

Count on the clock by 5s
to see how many minutes have passed.

___15___ minutes

after ___12___

___30___ minutes

after ___12___

___45___ minutes

after ___12___

Name_____

Telling Time

Can you speak **"clock time?"**

1. **"Quarter after"** means 15 minutes after the hour.

2. **"Half past"** means 30 minutes after the hour.

3. **"Quarter to"** means 15 minutes until the next hour.

Write the quarter-hours from this time.

_____ o'clock

quarter past _____

half past _____

quarter to _____

next hour: _____ o'clock

Name_____

Telling Time

Write the time on the digital clocks.

Name_____

Digital Clocks

Circle the correct digital time.

5:15
7:15

 11:30
9:30

 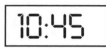
10:45
12:45

 9:45
3:45

 7:30
6:45

 10:00
2:00

 6:15
6:45

 10:30
10:45

 4:45
4:15

This pie bakes until a **quarter past 4.**

Name_____

Digital Clocks

Circle the correct digital time.

 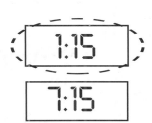
(1:15)
7:15

11:30
11:15

10:45
8:45

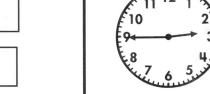 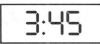
2:45
3:45

6:30
6:45

10:00
2:00

6:15
7:15

10:30
9:45

Digital Clocks

Write the time on the digital clocks.

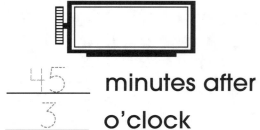

___45___ minutes after

___3___ o'clock

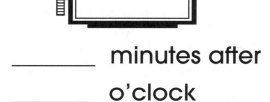

_____ minutes after

_____ o'clock

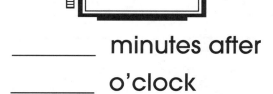

_____ minutes after

_____ o'clock

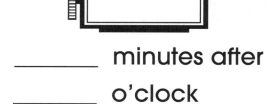

_____ minutes after

_____ o'clock

Time Two Ways

Draw the hands on each clock face. **Write the time.**

A. Marta **begins** writing a letter **at 3:30.** She **stops 30 minutes later.**

Begins

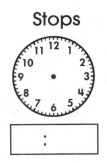

Stops

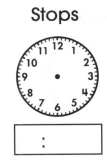

☐ : ☐   ☐ : ☐

B. Arnold **begins** drying dishes **at 8:00.** He **stops 15 minutes later.**

Begins

Stops

☐ : ☐   ☐ : ☐

C. Write your own time story.

_____

_____

_____

Begins   Stops

☐ : ☐   ☐ : ☐

Time Two Ways

Draw the hands on each clock face. **Write the time.**

A. Darius **begins** throwing balls for the dog **at 5:00**. He **stops 15 minutes later**.

Begins   Stops

[:]   [:]

B. Olga **begins** playing frisbee **at 4:15**. She **stops 15 minutes later**.

Begins   Stops

[:]   [:]

C. Write your own story.

_____

_____

_____

Begins   Stops

[:]   [:]

Name_____

Time Two Ways

Draw the hands on each clock face. **Write the time.**

A. Alberto **begins** working in the yard **at 10:00**. He **stops 45 minutes later.**

Begins

[:]

Stops

[:]

B. Darlene **begins** playing catch **at 2:30**. She **stops 15 minutes later.**

Begins

[:]

Stops

[:]

C. Write your own time story.

_____

_____

_____

Begins

[:]

Stops

[:]

Time Two Ways

Draw the hands on each clock face. **Write the time.**

A. Lucia **begins** practicing for the play **at 3:00**. She **stops 45 minutes later**.

Begins

:

Stops

:

B. Ann **begins** sorting her baseball cards **at 7:30**. She **stops 15 minutes later**.

Begins

:

Stops

:

C. Solve this time puzzle.
Ray biked **for 30 minutes**. He stopped biking **at 5:30**.
When did Ray begin biking?

Begins

:

Stops

:

Name_____

Time Two Ways

Draw the hands on each clock face. **Write the time.**

A. Jake **begins** playing a game **at 1:30**. He **stops 45 minutes later**.

Begins

Stops

[__ : __]

[__ : __]

B. Nicole **begins** swim practice **at 4:45**. She **stops 15 minutes later**.

Begins

Stops

[__ : __]

[__ : __]

C. **Solve this time puzzle.**

Jill worked in the recycling center **for 45 minutes**. She stopped working **at 7:45**. When did Jill begin working in the recycling center?

Begins

Stops

[__ : __]

[__ : __]

Time to the Minute Intervals: Introduction

Each number on the clock face **stands for 5 minutes.**

Count by 5s beginning at 12
Write the numbers here:

___0___ ___5___ ___10___ ___15___ ___20___ ___25___

It is __25__ minutes after __8__ o'clock. **It is written 8:25.**

Count by 5s. Fill in the blanks.

___0___ ____ ____ ____ ____ ____ ____ ____

It is _____ minutes after _____ o'clock,

or _____ : _____

Time to the Minute Intervals: Introduction

Count by 5s. Write the time both ways.

0 _____ _____

_____ minutes after _____ o'clock

_____ : _____

0 _____ _____ _____ _____

_____ minutes after _____ o'clock

_____ : _____

0 _____ _____ _____ _____

_____ _____

_____ minutes after _____ o'clock

_____ : _____

0 _____ _____ _____ _____ _____

_____ _____ _____ _____ _____

_____ minutes after _____ o'clock

_____ : _____

Circle the clocks with times **between 8 o'clock and 9 o'clock.**

Time to the Minute Intervals: Introduction

Count by 5s. Write the time both ways.

0 _____ _____ _____

_____ minutes after _____ o'clock

_____ : _____

0 _____ _____ _____ _____

_____ minutes after _____ o'clock

_____ : _____

---

0 _____ _____ _____ _____

_____ _____

_____ minutes after _____ o'clock

_____ : _____

---

0 _____ _____ _____ _____ _____

_____ _____ _____ _____ _____

_____ minutes after _____ o'clock

_____ : _____

Drawing the Minute Hand

This clock lost its minute hand! Can you help it? **Read the time**.

Trace the BIG HAND with a **red** crayon.

2:05

____5____ minutes after ____2____ o'clock

Drawing the Minute Hand

Draw each minute hand.

12:25

11:15

5:30

1:20

3:50

10:35

Name_____

Drawing the Minute Hand

Draw the hands on these fish clocks.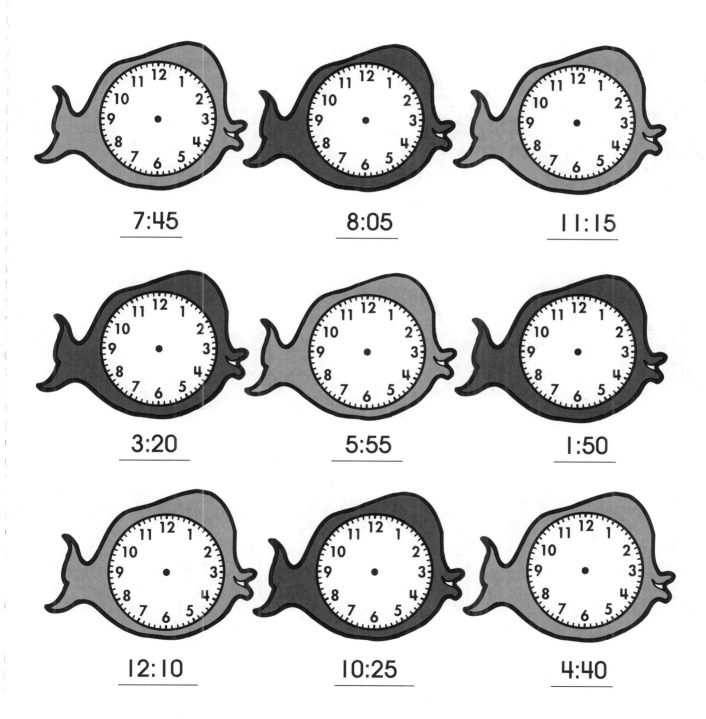

7:45

8:05

11:15

3:20

5:55

1:50

12:10

10:25

4:40

Name_____

Drawing the Minute Hand

Draw the hands on these fish clocks.

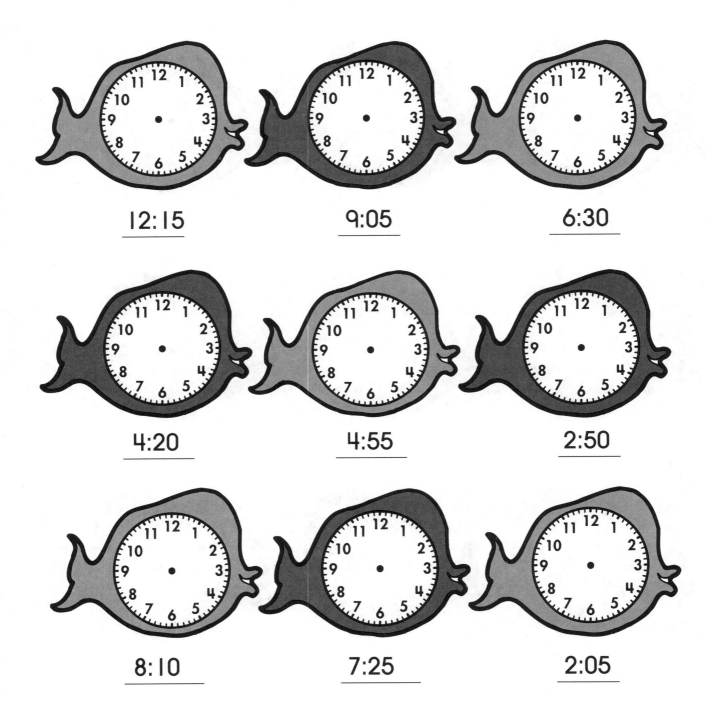

12:15   9:05   6:30

4:20   4:55   2:50

8:10   7:25   2:05

Name_____

Drawing the Minute Hand

Draw the hands on each clock to show the time you watch the cartoons.

Space Bunny
7:35

Car Wars
8:45

The Snuffs
5:15

Fun Runner
9:00

Scare Bears
2:40

Magic Elf
11:30

Tummy Bears
3:20

Monster Time
12:10

Sunny Funnies
1:05

What is your favorite cartoon?

_____

What time does it come on?

_____

Name_____

Digital Clocks

Read the digital clock. **First, read** the hour. **Then, read** the minutes.

This clock reads **four twenty** or
20 minutes past 4 o'clock.

Match the digital and face clocks.

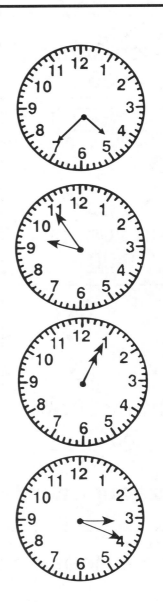

Digital Clocks

Match the digital and face clocks.

Digital Clocks

Circle the words that match each time.

five twenty  five fifty

six twenty-five  six thirty-five

seven ten  seven twenty

one fifty-five  eleven fifty-five

Matching Digital and Face Clocks

- -

Cut out each time and **glue** it under the correct face clock.

12:35	8:40	4:15	9:55	10:05
6:10	1:45	12:20	2:45	3:25

Page is blank for cutting
exercise on previous page.

Matching Digital and Face Clocks

Cut out each time and glue it under the correct clock.

7:40	1:05	4:20	3:55	11:10
6:25	12:45	2:20	5:05	8:25

Page is blank for cutting
exercise on previous page.

Name_____

Writing the Time

Write the times on the worms.

Writing the Time

Write the time below each clock.

_____

_____

_____

_____

_____

_____

_____

_____

_____

_____

_____

_____

Drawing Clock Hands

Draw the hands on each clock. **Write** each time.

Three thirty

Five forty-five

Eleven twenty

Eight ten

Two fifty-five

Nine forty

Drawing Clock Hands

Draw the hands on each clock. **Write** each time.

One oh-five

Three fifteen

Six fifty-five

Seven fifty

Four twenty-five

Five thirty

Time Two Ways

Draw the hands on each clock face.

Write the time.

A. 30 minutes after 6:00

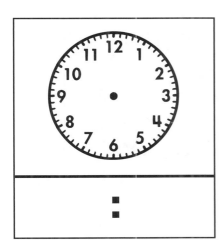

B. 20 minutes before 6:00

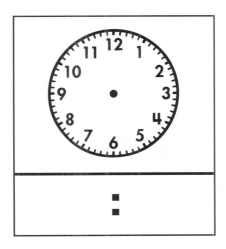

C. Exactly 6 o'clock

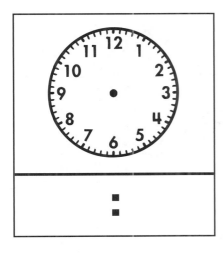

D. 20 minutes after 6:00

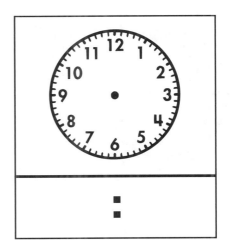

Name_____

Time Two Ways

Draw the hands on each face clock.

Write the time.

A. 25 minutes after 6:00

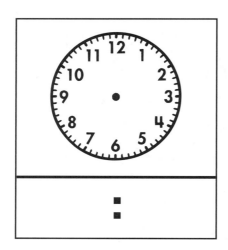

B. 15 minutes before 6:00

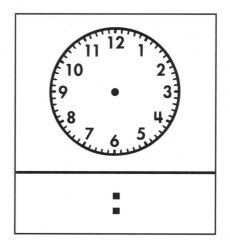

C. Exactly 7 o'clock

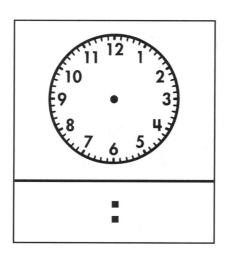

D. 35 minutes after 6:00

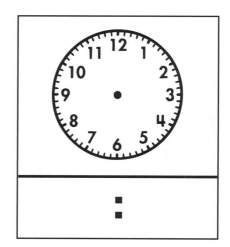

Name_____

Time Two Ways

Draw the hands on each face clock.

Write the time.

A. Exactly 12 o'clock

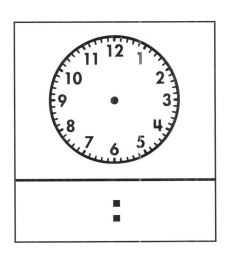

B. Quarter after 12:00

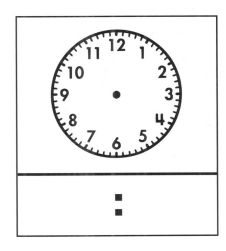

C. 15 minutes before 12:00

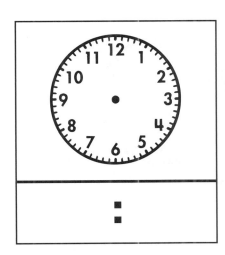

D. Half past 12:00

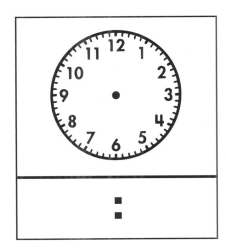

Name_____

Time Two Ways

Draw the hands on each face clock.

Write the time. ✏️

A. Exactly 3 o'clock

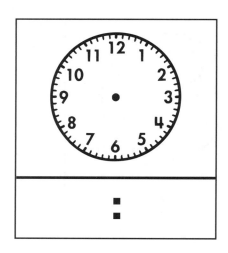

B. Quarter after 3:00

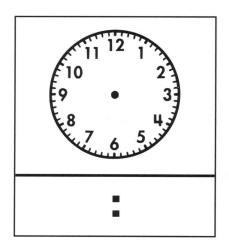

C. 20 minutes before 3:00

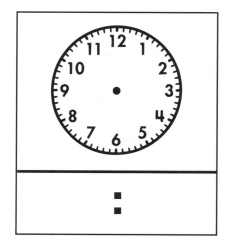

D. Half past 3:00

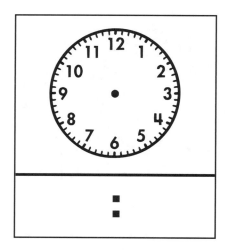

Name_____

Time Two Ways

Draw the hands on each face clock.

Write the time.

A. 2 hours past 12:00

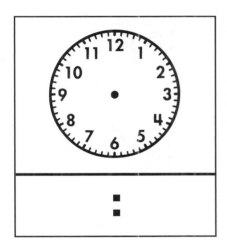

B. 10 minutes after 2:00

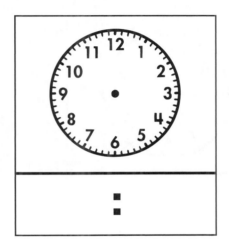

C. 45 minutes after 2:00

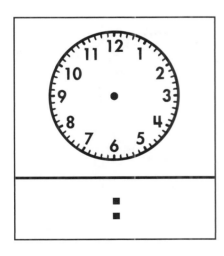

D. 50 minutes before 3:00

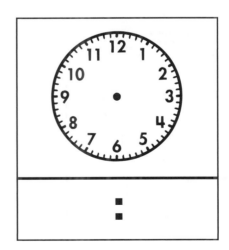

Name_____

Time Two Ways

Draw the hands on each clock face.

Write the time.

A. 3 hours past 8:00

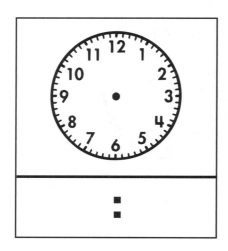

B. 30 minutes after 11:00

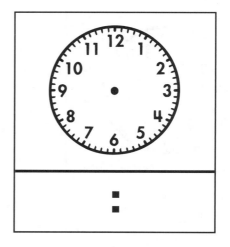

C. 25 minutes after 11:00

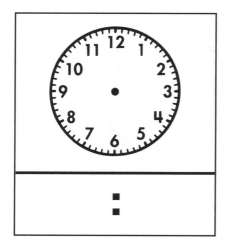

D. 30 minutes before 12:00

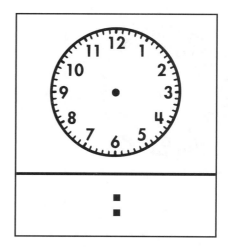

Name_____

Writing Familiar Times

Write the time. **Draw** the hands on each clock.

I get up at _____.   I go to bed at _____.   Lunch is at _____.

Dinner is at _____.   School starts at _____.   School ends at _____.

Recess is at _____.   I play at _____.

Time Lapse: Minutes

How much time did each school picnic activity take?

1. Jimmy played darts from 1:20 till 1:40.
   He played for _____20_____ minutes.

2. Marietta rode a pony for 15 minutes.
   She began at 1:00.
   She finished at _____ : _____.

3. She had so much fun, she rode
   another 15 minutes.
   She finished at _____ : _____ .

Time Lapse: Minutes

4. Tim worked at the snow cone booth. The first clock shows the time he started. He worked for 1 hour and 30 minutes. **Draw the time** he finished on the second clock.

5. Andrea won the juggling contest. She kept the balls in the air for 5 minutes. She began juggling at 1:25. She finished at _____ : _____.
Circle the clock that shows the time she finished.

Write the time.

_____   _____   _____

Name_____

Drawing Clock Hands

Read each story.

Draw the hands on each clock face.

A. Frog sees a fly at 1:00. He catches the fly and eats it 45 minutes later.

Sees fly　　　　　　**Eats fly**

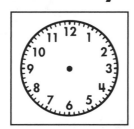　　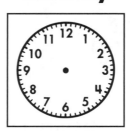　　

B. Frog hops out of the water at 2:00.
Frog hops back in the water 40 minutes later.

Hops out　　　　**Hops back in**

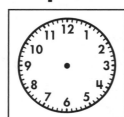　　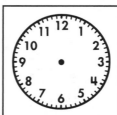

C. Frog sits on a lily pad at 3:00.
He swims away 45 minutes later.

Sits on lily pad　　**Swims away**

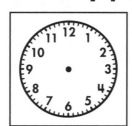　　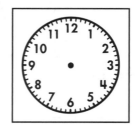

Drawing Clock Hands

Read each story.

Draw the hands on each clock face.

A. Rabbit hops into his garden at 6:00. He finishes working in the garden one and one-half hours later.

Hops in garden   **Finishes work**

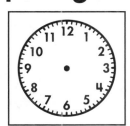      

B. Rabbit cooks lettuce and carrots at 8:30. He finishes eating 45 minutes later.

Cooks lettuce & carrots   **Finishes eating**

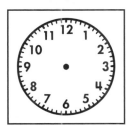   

C. Rabbit lies down for a nap at 4:00. He wakes up and hops away 55 minutes later.

Lies down   **Wakes up**

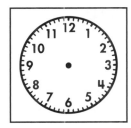   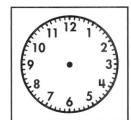

Drawing Clock Hands

Read each story.

Draw the hands on each clock face.

A. Pig takes a mud bath at 9:00.
Pig showers 15 minutes later.

Takes mud bath   **Showers**

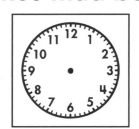 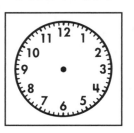 

B. On Monday, Pig begins cleaning at 12:00.
Her house is clean 90 minutes later.

Begins cleaning   **House is clean**

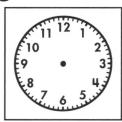 

C. On Tuesday, Pig goes to the market at 12:45.
She comes home with a basket full of goodies 30 minutes later.

Goes to market   **Comes home**

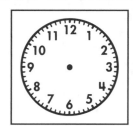 

Time Stories

Read the story. **Write** each time.

Val and Phil go out to the backyard at 6:00. They put up their tent. This takes them 1 hour and 30 minutes. They get in the tent and talk for 1 hour. Then they fall asleep. They sleep for 2 hours, until a dog barks and wakes them up.

A. Go to backyard

B. Finish putting up tent

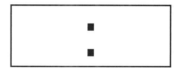

C. Fall asleep

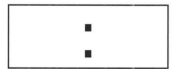

D. Dog barks

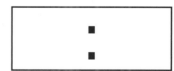

E. How long are Val and Phil in the yard before the dog wakes them up?

_____ hours _____ minutes

Time Stories

Read the story. **Write** each time.

Mike and Maria leave home at 3:30. They ride their bikes to the ice-skating rink. This takes one half-hour. They skate and leave the rink 2 hours later. They get on their bikes and arrive home 40 minutes after leaving the rink.

A. Leave home

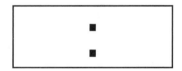

B. Arrive at rink

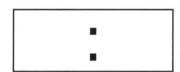

C. Leave rink

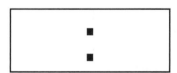

D. Arrive home

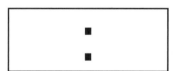

E. How long does Mike and Maria's trip to the skating rink and back take?

_____ hours _____ minutes

Time Stories

Read the story. **Write** each time.

Joe and José put on roller skates at 8:30. They skate for 2 hours, then stop to rest. They rest for one half-hour, then start skating again. They reach the park 1 hour and 45 minutes later.

A. Put on roller skates

B. Stop to rest

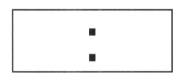

C. Start skating again

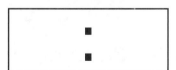

D. Arrive at park

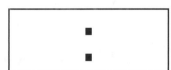

E. How long does Joe and José's trip to the park take?

_____ hours _____ minutes

Name_____

Time Stories

Read the story. **Write** each time.

Andrea took her dog for a walk. They left home at 5:30. They walked for 20 minutes. What time did they get home?

A. Leave home

B. Get home

Rhiannon and her mother made cookies. They put the cookies in the oven at 7:15. After 10 minutes they took the cookies out of the oven. Yum! What time did they take them out?

C. Cookies in oven

D. Cookies out of oven

Anita played table tennis with her brother for 30 minutes. They stopped playing at 4:30. When did Anita begin playing table tennis?

E. Begin playing

F. Stop playing

Time Stories

Read each story. **Write** each time.

Benito went for a ride on the roller coaster. He got on the roller coaster at 2:30. He rode for 15 minutes. What time did he get off?

A. Start ride

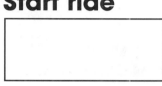

B. Get off

Valerie and her sister went hiking. They started hiking at 9:00. They hiked for one hour and 30 minutes. What time did they stop hiking?

C. Start hike

D. Finish hike

When did Ben and his mother get on the subway? Ben and his mother rode the subway for 20 minutes. They got off the subway at 4:30.

E. Get on

F. Get off

Time Stories

Read the story. **Write** each time.

Andrea and her sister walked by the lake. They started walking at 2:15. They walked for one hour and 15 minutes. What time did they stop walking?

A. Start walking

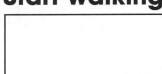

B. Stop walking

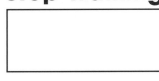

Berta gave her dog Maria a bath. She started washing Maria at 7:40. Maria hates baths. It took Berta 50 minutes to wash the dog. They both got wet! When did she finish?

C. Start bath

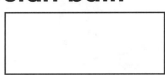

D. Finish bath

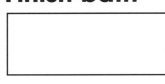

Sergei played disc golf with his sister for 40 minutes. They stopped playing at 7:30. When did Sergei start playing disc golf?

E. Begin playing

F. Stop playing

156 *Complete Book of Time & Money • Grades K-3*

Time Stories

Read the story. **Write** each time.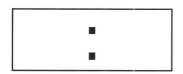

Erin and her brother Harry were shopping for dinner. First they went into the bakery at 5:00 to buy fresh bread. This took 5 minutes. Next they walked to the market for vegetables and cereal. This took them 20 minutes. Then they walked next door for a treat at Fanny's Famous Fudge. This took them 15 minutes. Then they met their brother Andrew outside.

A. Go into bakery

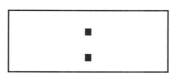

B. Leave bakery

C. Leave market

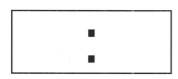

D. Meet Andrew

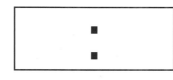

E. How long had Erin and Harry been shopping before they saw Andrew?

_____

F. Write your own story about shopping on another sheet of paper. What do you do, and how long does each thing take? Make up a starting time. Use a clock to find the ending time.

Time Stories

Read the story. Write each time.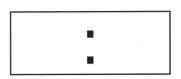

Hanna and Shawn got to the fair at 3:00. They threw balls at the clown's pocket for 10 minutes. No luck! Then they rode the Big Dipper for 30 minutes. They got wet! After this they ate pizza for 15 minutes. Then they saw their friend Mary.

A. Arrive at the fair

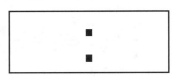

B. Stop throwing balls

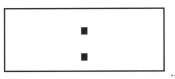

C. Stop riding Big Dipper

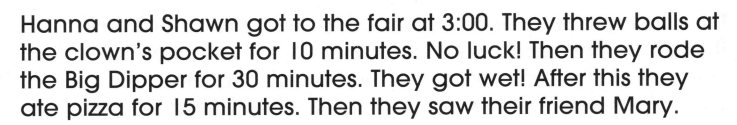

D. See Mary

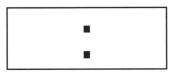

E. How long had Hanna and Shawn been at the fair before they saw Mary?

_____

F. Write your own story about being at the fair on another sheet of paper. What do you do, and how long does each thing take? Make up a starting time. Use your clock to find the ending time.

Time Stories

Read the story. **Write** each time.

Valerie and Angela got off the bus at the mall. It was 12:30. First they went to Toby's Toys & Games. They looked at toys for 20 minutes. Then they spent 40 minutes walking to Yummy Yogurt and having a snack. Then they looked at shoes in The Shoe Factory for 15 minutes. They met Angela's sister outside the Shoe Factory.

A. Arrive at mall

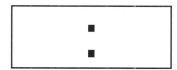

B. Leave toy store

C. Leave Yummy Yogurt

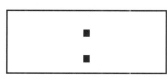

D. See Angela's sister

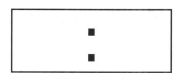

E. **How long** had Valerie and Angela been at the mall when they saw Angela's sister?

_____

F. **Write** your own story about shopping on another sheet of paper. What do you do, and how long does each thing take? Make up a starting time. Use your clock to find the ending time.

Name_____

Time Puzzles

Write times that fit each time clue.

A. Between 11:00 and 12:00

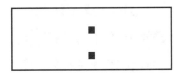

B. Between 30 minutes after 2:00 and 3:00

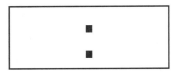

7:15 is my bedtime.

C. After a quarter-past 7:00 and before 8:00

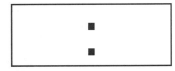

D. **Write** your own time clues.
   Ask a friend to solve your time puzzle!

_____

_____

_____

Name_____

Time Puzzles

Write times that fit each time clue.

A. Between 4:15 and 5:15

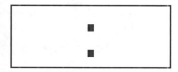

B. After 6:00 and before a quarter to 7:00

Time to brush my teeth!

C. Between 12:00 and 1:00

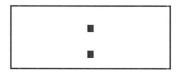

D. **Write** your own time clues.
Ask a friend to solve your time puzzle!

_____

_____

_____

Name_____

Time Puzzles

Write times that fit each time clue.

A. After 3:00 and before 3:40

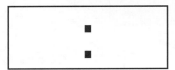

B. Between a quarter after 1:00 and 3:00

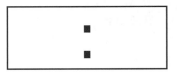

C. Before 9:00 and after 8:20

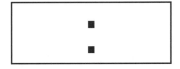

D. **Write** your own time clues.
Ask a friend to solve your time puzzle!

It's lunchtime!

11:15

_____

_____

_____

Telling Time: Using Charts

BIG TEN MOVIES:

Mark's Great Adventure	12:15	3:00	5:30
The Mad Hatter Returns	12:45	3:30	5:45
Morris and the Magic Van	1:30	4:15	6:45

Use the chart. Find the movie that each pair saw.

Write the time that the movie started.

A. Barry and his brother went to the movie that began closest to 4:00.

Movie: _____

Began at: _____

B. Andrea and her friend went to the movie that began closest to 1:00.

Movie: _____

Began at: _____

C. Ismelda and her mom went to the movie that began closest to 6:00.

Movie: _____

Began at: _____

D. **Write** your own time puzzle about Big Ten Movies on another sheet of
paper. Ask a friend to solve your time puzzle.

Name_____

Telling Time: Using Charts

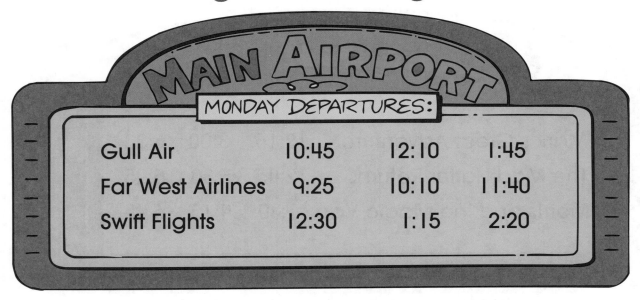

MAIN AIRPORT

MONDAY DEPARTURES:

Gull Air	10:45	12:10	1:45
Far West Airlines	9:25	10:10	11:40
Swift Flights	12:30	1:15	2:20

Use the chart. Find the airline that each pair used.

Write the time that the flight left.

A. Teresa and her aunt flew on the plane that left closest to 10:30.

Airline: _____

Left at: _____

B. Kelly and her mother flew on the plane that left closest to 11:00.

Airline: _____

Left at: _____

C. Leticia and her father flew on the plane that left closest to 12:15.

Airline: _____

Left at: _____

D. **Write** your own time puzzle about the Main Airport on another sheet of paper. Ask a friend to solve your time puzzle.

Name_____

Telling Time: Using Charts

BAYSIDE AQUARIUM

SATURDAY FEEDINGS:

Otters	2:00	3:30	5:00
Dolphins	11:30	3:15	5:20
Sharks	2:30	4:00	5:45

Use the chart. Find the animal that each pair saw.

Write the time that the animal was fed.

A. Francisco and José went to the feeding that was closest to 3:00.

Animal: _____

Feeding at: _____

B. Alex and Shannon went to the feeding that was closest to 6:00.

Animal: _____

Feeding at: _____

C. Kim and Amanda went to the feeding that was closest to 5:30.

Animal: _____

Feeding at: _____

D. **Write** your own time puzzle about the Bayside Aquarium on another sheet of paper. Ask a friend to solve your time puzzle.

MONEY

Pennies: Introduction

This is a **penny**.

It is worth **1 cent.**
It has **2 sides.**

 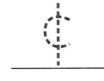

front   back

This is the **cent symbol.**
Trace it.

 _____

Color the pennies **brown.**

Pennies: Introduction

Find each penny. **Color** it brown.

How many pennies did you find? _____

Name_____

Counting Pennies

Count the pennies.

_____ pennies = _____ ¢

_____ pennies = _____ ¢

_____ penny = _____ ¢

Counting Pennies

Count the pennies.

_____ pennies = _____ ¢

_____ pennies = _____ ¢

_____ pennies = _____ ¢

Name_____

Counting Pennies

Each piece of candy costs 1¢.

Cut out each money box and **glue** it beside the candy it will buy.

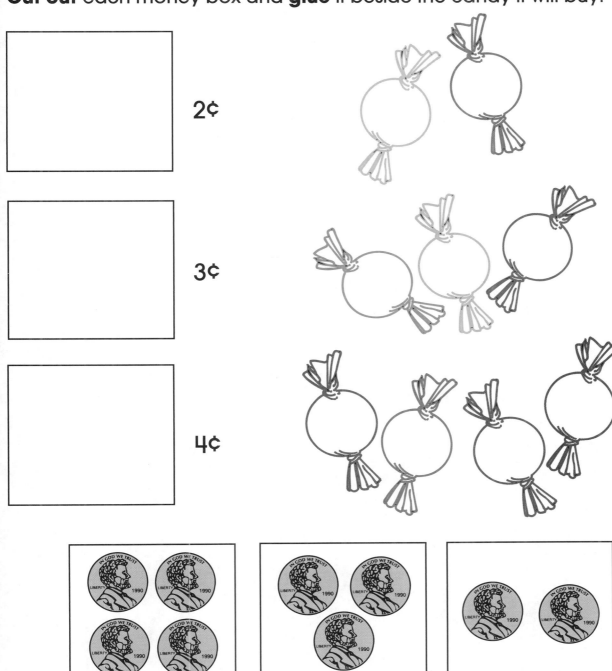

2¢

3¢

4¢

Page is blank for cutting
exercise on previous page.

Counting Pennies

I penny = I ¢

How much money is there?

Example:

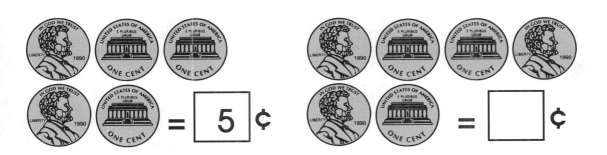

= 5 ¢

= ☐ ¢

= ☐ ¢

= ☐ ¢

Counting Pennies

1 penny = 1 ¢

How much money is there?

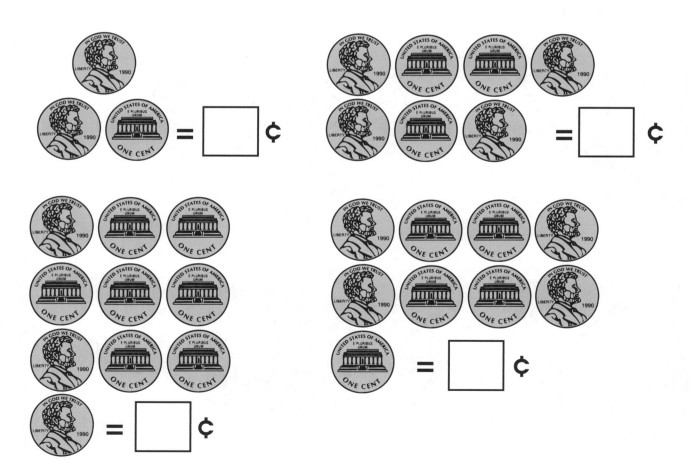

Name_____

Counting Pennies

Count the pennies.

How many cents are there?

Example:

 = | 4 | ¢

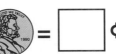 = ☐ ¢

 = ☐ ¢

 = ☐ ¢

 = ☐ ¢

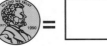 = ☐ ¢

 = ☐ ¢

 = ☐ ¢

 = ☐ ¢

Name_____

Counting Pennies

Count the pennies on each flower.

Write the number of cents in the center.

Example:

Counting Pennies

Penny Pinchers

Draw a line from each group of pennies to the correct number of cents.

Example:

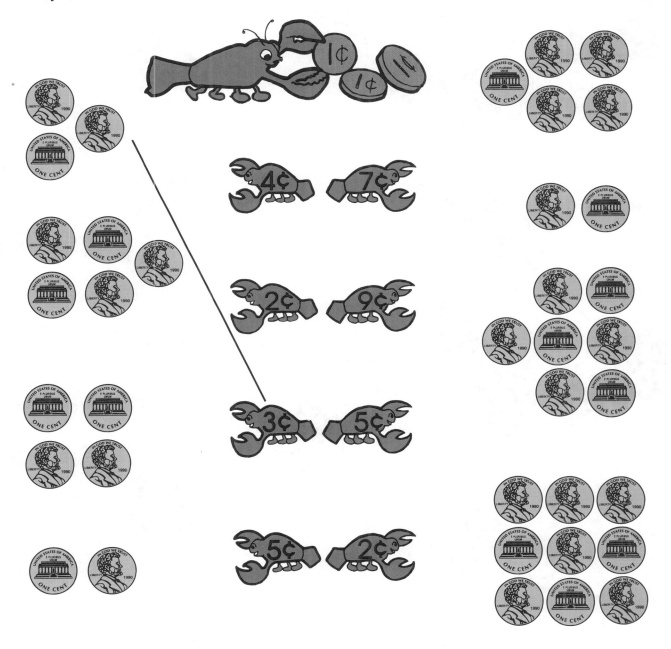

Name_____

Counting Pennies

Count the pennies in each chain.

Draw a line to the correct number of cents.

2¢

3¢

5¢

6¢

Name_____

Counting Pennies

Count the pennies in each chain.

Draw a line to the correct number of cents. ✏️

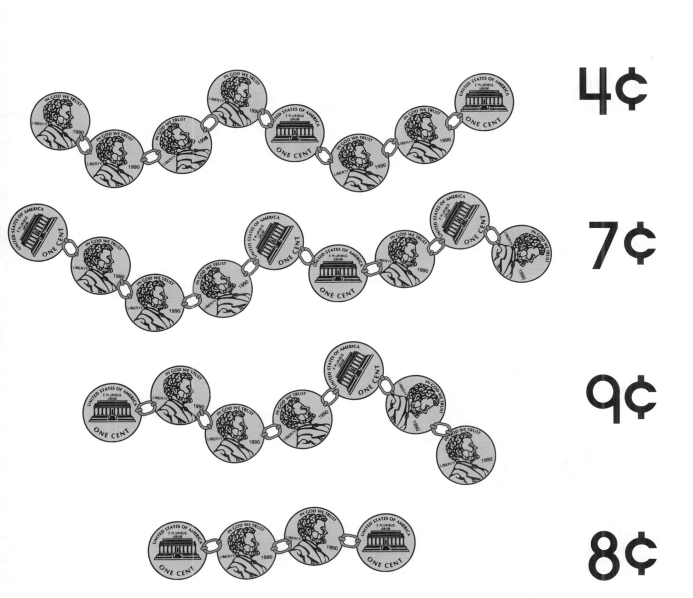

4¢

7¢

9¢

8¢

Name_____

Counting Pennies

Count the pennies in each triangle.

_____ ¢

_____ ¢

_____ ¢

Name_____

Counting Pennies

Write the number of cents on each bag.

Color each penny.

Name_____

Counting Pennies

Write the number of cents on each bag.

Color each penny.

Name_____

Counting Pennies

Count the pennies in each group.

Match each group to the correct bag.

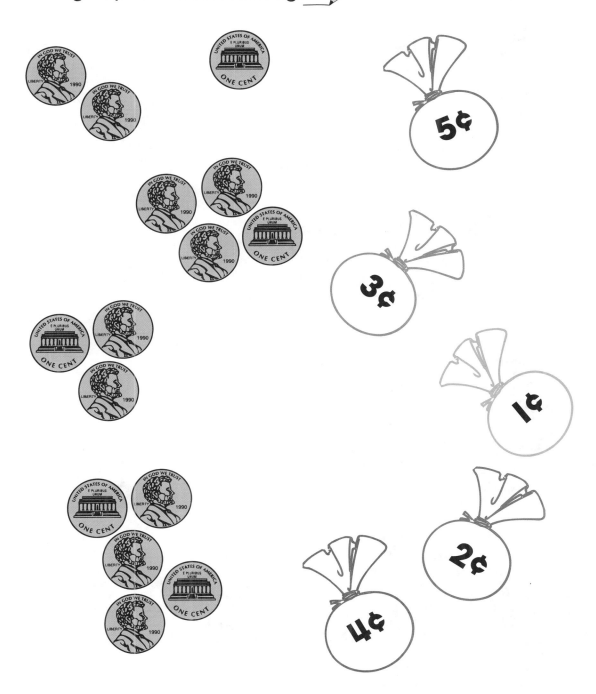

Counting Pennies

Count the pennies in each group.

Match each group to the correct bag.

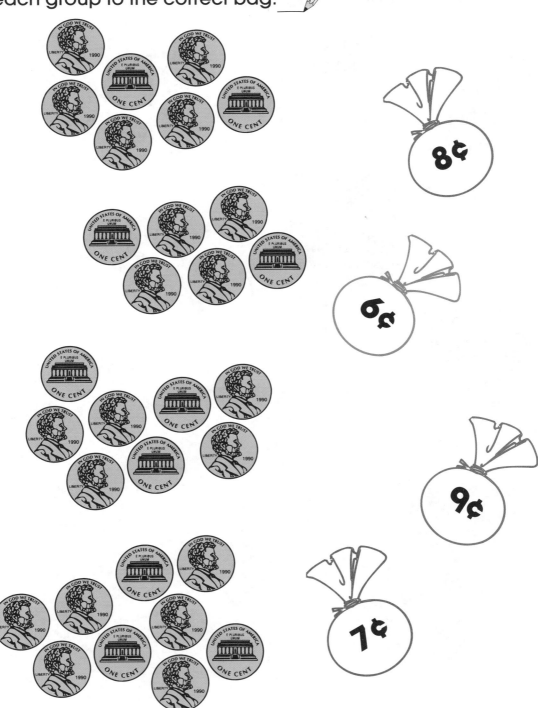

Name_____

Counting Pennies

Count the pennies on each ride.

Write the number of pennies on the line.

Color each ride.

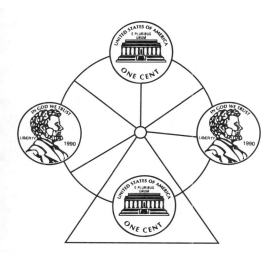

_____ ¢

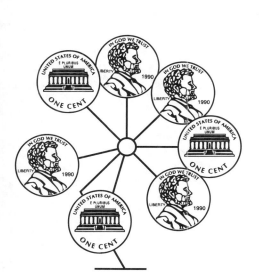

_____ ¢

Name_____

Counting Pennies

Count the pennies on each ride.

Write the number of pennies on the line.

Color each ride.

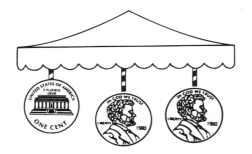

_____ ¢

_____ ¢

_____ ¢

Name_____

Counting Pennies

Count the pennies in each piggy bank.

Write the number of pennies.

_____ ¢

_____ ¢

Name_____

Counting Pennies

Count the pennies in each piggy bank.

Write the number of pennies.

_____ ¢

_____ ¢

Counting Pennies

Count the pennies in each hand.

Write the number of pennies.

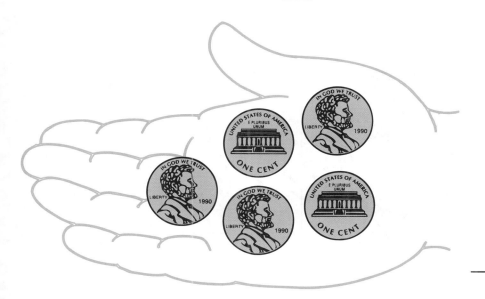

_____¢

_____¢

Name_____

Counting Pennies

Count the pennies in each hand.

Write the number of pennies.

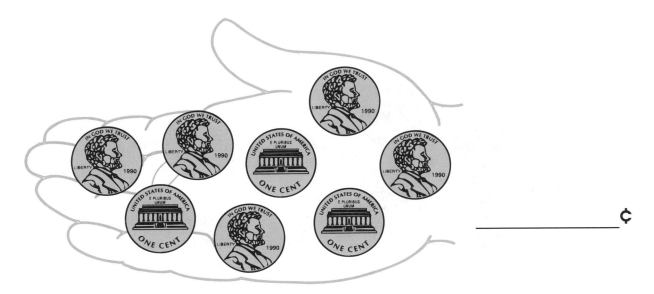

_____ ¢

_____ ¢

Counting Pennies

Count the pennies on each animal.

Write the number of pennies.

 ¢

_____ ¢

Circle the animal that has more money.

Name_____

Counting Pennies

Count the pennies on each animal.

Write the number of pennies. _____

_____ ¢

_____ ¢

Circle the animal
that has more money.

Nickels: Introduction

Color the nickels silver.

front   back

_____ nickel   =   _____ pennies

_____ nickel   =   _____ cents

_____ nickel   =   _____ ¢

5¢ = ____¢ + ____¢ + ____¢ + ____¢ + ____¢

Counting with Nickels and Pennies

A **nickel** is worth **5¢**.

Count the money in each bag.

Write how much money is in the bag.

A.

_____¢

B.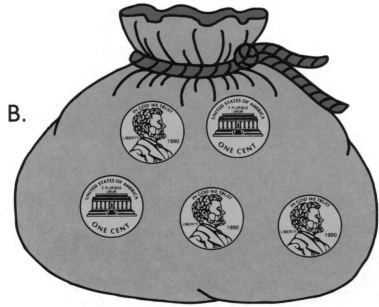

_____¢

Both of these bags hold 5¢!

Counting with Nickels and Pennies

You can count pennies and nickels together!

Remember: They each have a front and a back!

Here are both sides of a **penny**.
Color them **brown**.

And here are both sides of a **nickel**.
Color them **silver**.

I penny = _____ cent

I penny = _____ ¢

I nickel = _____ cents

I nickel = _____ ¢

Draw the cent symbol here: _____

Name_____

Counting with Nickels and Pennies

Count the money.

Say 5 for the nickel and **add** I for each penny. **Write** each amount.

I.		= _____7_____ ¢
2.		= _____ ¢
3.		= _____ ¢
4.		= _____ ¢

Name_____

Counting with Nickels and Pennies

Count the money.

Write each amount.

 _____¢

 _____¢

 _____¢

 _____¢

 _____¢

 _____¢

Name_____

Counting with Nickels and Pennies

Count the money. **Start** with the nickel. Then, **count** the pennies.

Write each amount.

_____ ¢

_____ ¢

Name_____

Counting with Nickels and Pennies

Count the money. **Start** with the nickel. Then, **count** the pennies.

Write each amount.

_____ ¢

_____ ¢

Counting with Nickels and Pennies

Count the money.

Write each amount.

_____ ¢

_____ ¢

Circle the animal
that has more money.

Counting with Nickels and Pennies

Count the money.

Write each amount.

_____ ¢

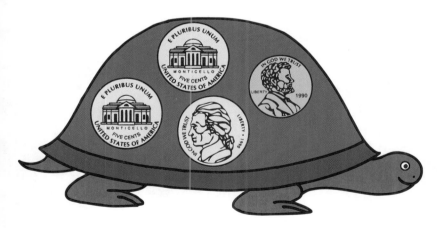

_____ ¢

Circle the animal
that has more money.

Counting with Nickels and Pennies

Write how much the nickels are worth.

 = _____ ¢

  = _____ ¢

= _____ ¢   = _____ ¢

 = _____ ¢

= _____ ¢

= _____ ¢   = _____ ¢

 = _____ ¢

= _____ ¢

= _____ ¢

= _____ ¢   = _____ ¢

Counting with Nickels and Pennies

Count the money.

Write each amount.

_____ ¢

_____ ¢

Circle the animal
that has more money.

Name_____

Counting with Nickels and Pennies

Count the money.

Write each amount.

_____ ¢

_____ ¢

Circle the animal
that has more money.

Nickels: Counting by Fives

Count by 5s.
Fill in the blanks.

_____ , _____ , _____ , _____ , _____ ,

_____ , _____ , _____ , _____ , _____ ,

_____ , _____ , _____ , _____ , _____ ,

_____ , _____ , _____ , _____ , _____ ,

This is how to count nickels!

Practice counting by 5s!

Name_____

Nickels: Counting by Fives

Count the nickels by 5s. **5¢ = 1 nickel**

Write the amount.

Example:

  15 ¢

    ☐ ¢

Count __5__, __10__, __15__ .   Count ____, ____.

☐ ¢

Count ____, ____, ____, ____, ____.   Count ____, ____, ____, ____, ____, ____, ____.

☐ ¢

☐ ¢

Count ____, ____, ____, ____.   Count ____, ____, ____, ____, ____, ____.

Name _____

Nickels: Counting by Fives

Count the money.

Write how much each clown is worth.

_____ ¢

_____ ¢

_____ ¢

_____ ¢

Name_____

Nickels: Counting by Fives

Count the money.

Write the amount on each meter.

Example:

Name_____

Nickels: Counting by Fives

Write how much money is in each hive.

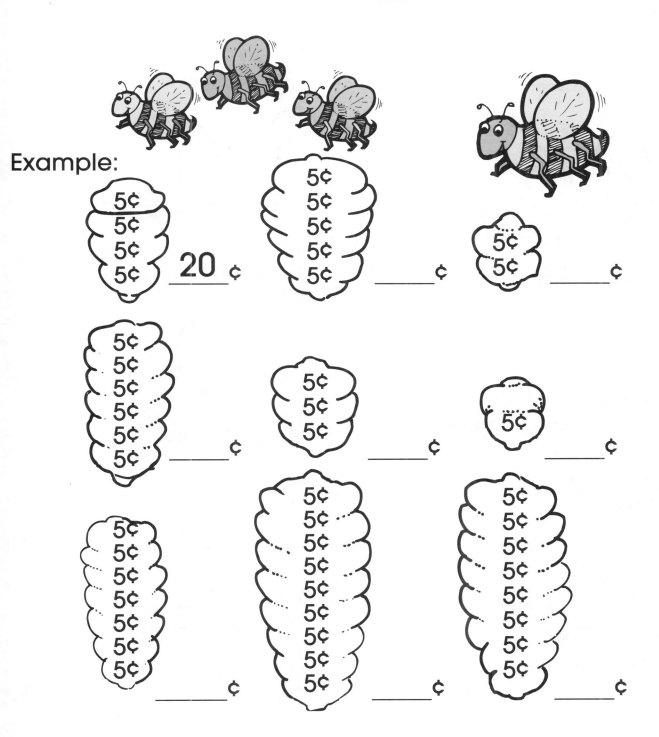

Example:

5¢
5¢
5¢
5¢   __20__ ¢

5¢
5¢
5¢
5¢
5¢   _____ ¢

5¢
5¢   _____ ¢

5¢
5¢
5¢
5¢
5¢
5¢   _____ ¢

5¢
5¢
5¢   _____ ¢

5¢   _____ ¢

5¢
5¢
5¢
5¢
5¢
5¢   _____ ¢

5¢
5¢
5¢
5¢
5¢
5¢
5¢
5¢
5¢   _____ ¢

5¢
5¢
5¢
5¢
5¢
5¢
5¢   _____ ¢

Name_____

Counting with Nickels and Pennies

Count the money.

Write the amount under each bunny's carrot.

Example:

Counting with Nickels and Pennies

Count the money.

Write the amount under each bunny's carrot.

Example:

6 ¢

_____ ¢

_____ ¢

_____ ¢

_____ ¢

_____ ¢

Name_____

Counting with Nickels and Pennies

Count the money. **Write** each amount.

Draw a line to match each owl with the same amount of money.

Example:

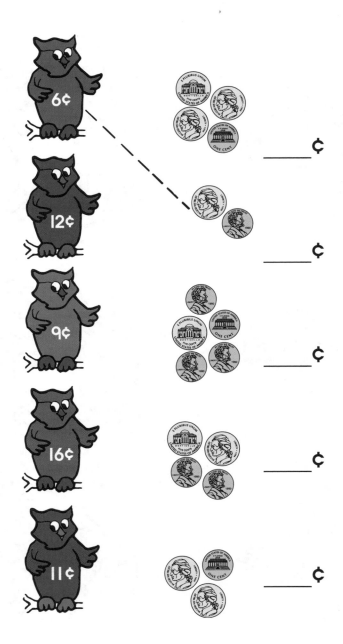

_____ ¢

_____ ¢

_____ ¢

_____ ¢

_____ ¢

Name_____

Counting with Nickels and Pennies

Count the money. **Write** each amount.

Draw a line to match each owl with the same amount of money.

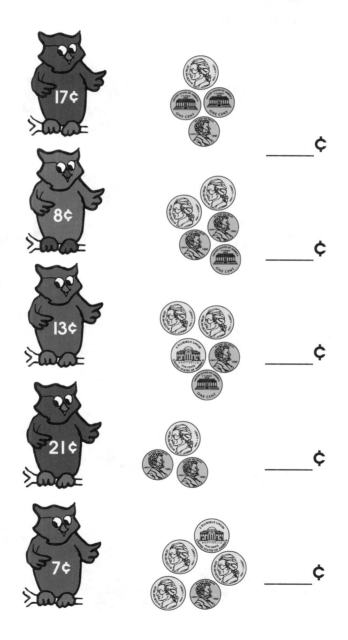

_____¢

_____¢

_____¢

_____¢

_____¢

Counting with Nickels and Pennies

Count the money on each "**cent**"-erpillar. **Write** each amount.

Example:

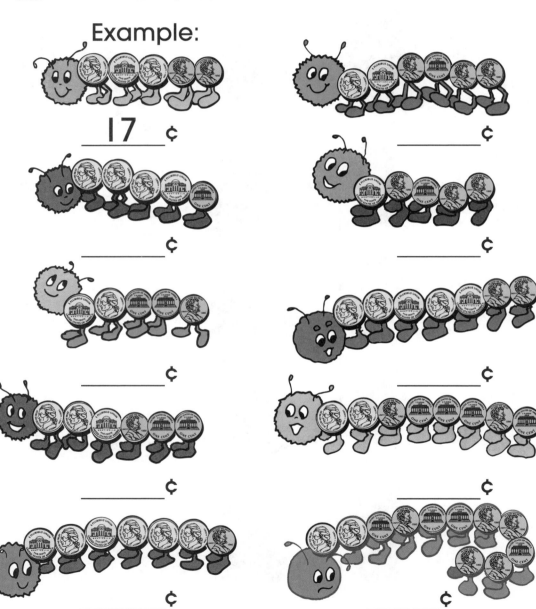

17 ¢

Name_____

Counting with Nickels and Pennies

Count the money on each "**cent**"-erpillar. **Write** each amount.

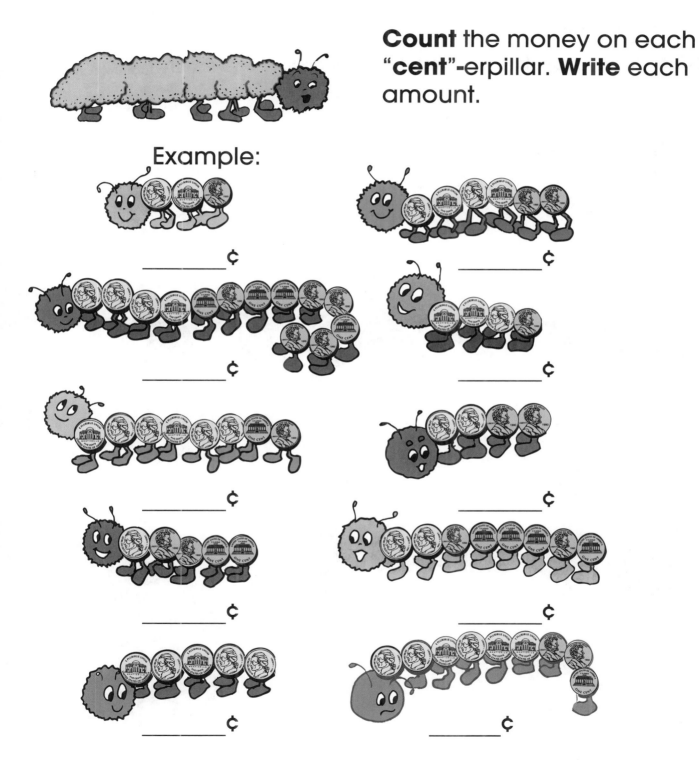

Example:

_____¢

_____¢

_____¢

_____¢

_____¢

_____¢

_____¢

_____¢

_____¢

_____¢

Counting with Nickels and Pennies

Count the money.

Start with the nickels. Then, **count** the pennies.

_____¢ _____¢ _____¢ _____¢ = _____¢
Total

____¢ ____¢ ____¢ ____¢ ____¢ ____¢ ____¢

= ____¢
Total

____¢ ____¢ ____¢ ____¢ ____¢

= ____¢
Total

Name_____

Counting with Nickels and Pennies

Count the money.

Start with the nickels. Then, **count** the pennies.

_____¢ _____¢ _____¢ = _____¢
                                    Total

_____¢ _____¢ _____¢ _____¢ _____¢ _____¢

= _____¢
   Total

_____¢ _____¢ _____¢ _____¢

= _____¢
   Total

Name_____

Counting with Nickels and Pennies

Look at the price on each toy.

Color the toy if there are enough nickels to buy it.

Name_____

Adding with Nickels and Pennies

Write how much money there is.

 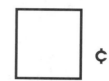

☐ ¢

+ ☐ ¢
_____
☐ ¢

 ☐ ¢ + ☐ ¢ = ☐ ¢

Adding with Nickels and Pennies

Write how much money there is.

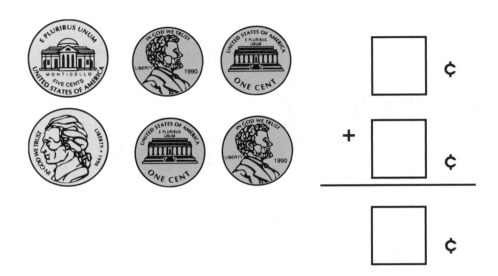

⬜ ¢

+ ⬜ ¢

⬜ ¢

Draw groups of pennies and nickels here.

Write an addition sentence using the coins you drew.

Color the coins.

Adding with Nickels and Pennies

Write an addition sentence for each problem.

Example:

 +

2¢ + 1¢ = 3¢

_____

 + _____ + _____ + _____

_____   _____   _____

 + _____ + _____ + _____

_____   _____   _____

 + _____ + _____ + _____

_____   _____   _____

Adding with Nickels and Pennies

Kristen is having a birthday party. Let's see what she bought for her 3 friends.

These are for her friends.

1. For Cassie, she bought the and the .

   She paid _____¢.

2. For Terri, she bought the and the ;

   She paid _____¢.

3. For Lauren, she bought the and the .

   She paid _____¢.

Adding with Nickels and Pennies

Every birthday party needs balloons.

Draw one for each girl, including Kristen.

The balloons cost 5¢ each. **Count** by 5s. Kristen paid _____ ¢.

She also bought bubble wands.
Draw one for each girl.

The wands cost 2¢ each. **Count** by 2s. Kristen paid _____ ¢.

Finally! It's time to open the presents!
Color the presents.

Name_____

Dimes: Introduction

The dime is small, but quite strong.
It can buy more than a penny or a nickel.

front   back

A dime has a front and a back. It has ridges on its edge.
Color the dime silver.

 =

Fill in the blanks.

_____ dime = _____ pennies

_____ dime = _____ cents

_____ dime = _____ ¢

Counting with Dimes and Pennies

Dimes are easy to count.

Start with the dime, then add the pennies. **Write** each amount.

 + = _____ ¢

_____ _____ _____

 +   = _____ ¢

_____ _____ _____ _____

 + = _____ ¢

_____ _____

 +   =

_____ _____ _____

 = _____ ¢

_____ _____ _____

Name_____

Counting with Dimes and Pennies

Count the money.

Write each amount.

_____¢

_____¢

Name_____

Counting with Dimes and Pennies

Count the money.

Write each amount.

_____¢

_____¢

Name_____

Dimes: Counting by Tens

Count by 10s.

Fill in the blanks.

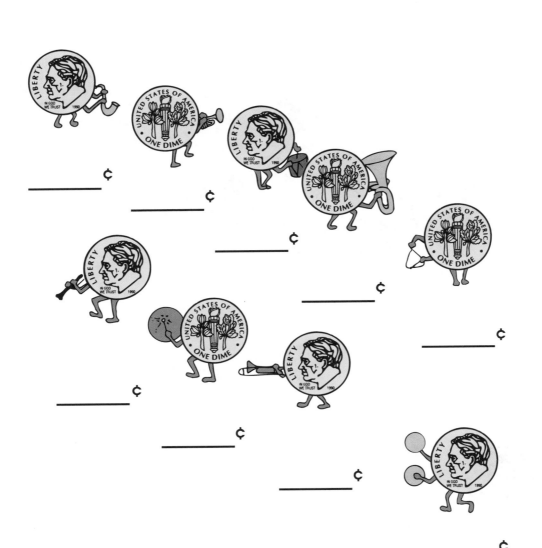

_____ ¢

_____ ¢

_____ ¢

_____ ¢

_____ ¢

_____ ¢

_____ ¢

_____ ¢

_____ ¢

_____ ¢

Name_____

Dimes: Counting by Tens

Count by 10s. **Write** each number.
Circle the group with more money.

_____¢   or   _____¢

_____¢   or   _____¢

_____¢   or   _____¢

Name_____

Counting with Dimes and Pennies

Count the dimes by tens. Then, **count** the pennies.

Write each amount.

Example:

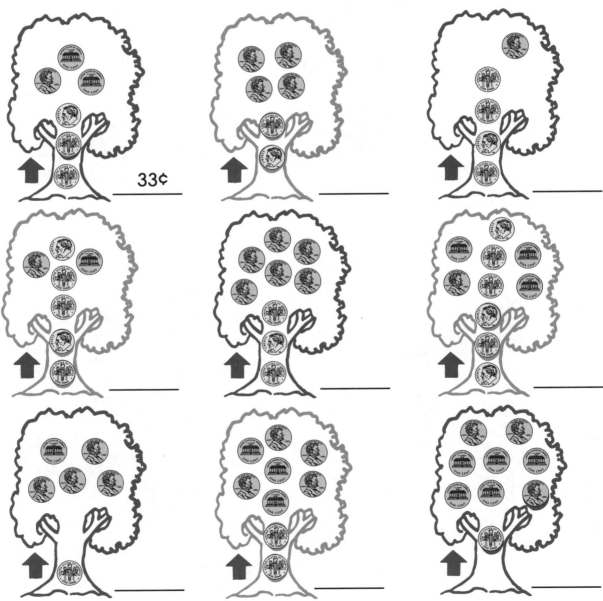

33¢

Name_____

Counting with Dimes and Pennies

Count the dimes by tens. Then, **count** the pennies.

Write each amount.

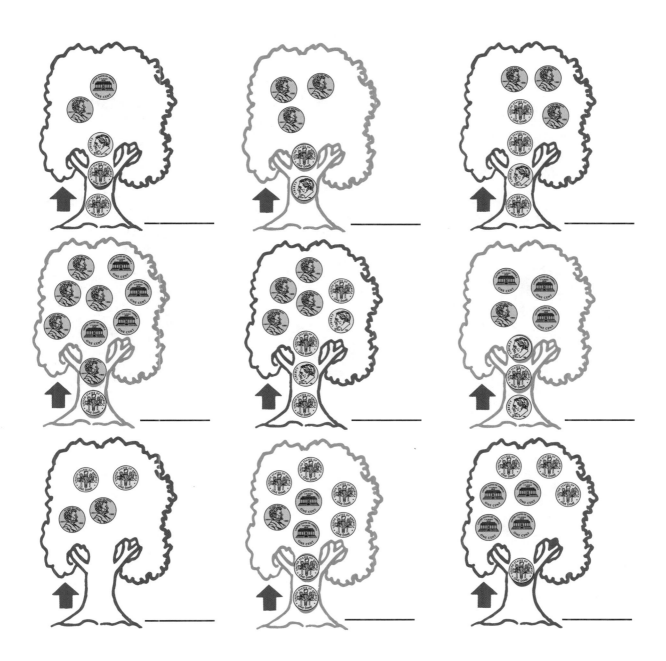

Name_____

Counting with Dimes and Nickels

Look carefully at the dimes and nickels.
Circle two nickels, then two more,
until all the nickels are circled.

Then, **count** by 10s to see how much money there is.

There is _____ ¢

Name_____

Counting with Dimes and Nickels

Count the money.

Write each amount.

_____ ¢   _____ ¢   _____ ¢   _____ ¢   _____ ¢   _____ ¢

Total

_____ ¢   _____ ¢   _____ ¢   _____ ¢   _____ ¢   _____ ¢

_____ ¢   _____ ¢   _____ ¢   _____ ¢

Total

What coins does Raccoon have?

I'm counting my money.
10¢, 20¢, 30¢, 35¢,
40¢, 45¢, 50¢...

Name_____

Counting with Dimes, Nickels, and Pennies

Count the money.

Write each amount.

_____ ¢

_____ ¢

Circle the animal
that has more money.

Name_____

Counting with Dimes, Nickels, and Pennies

Count the money.

Write each amount.

_____ ¢

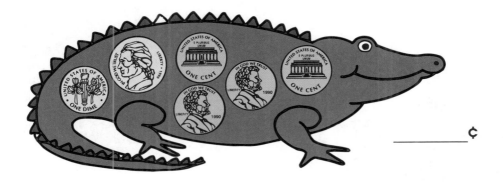

_____ ¢

Circle the animal
that has more money.

Name_____

Counting with Dimes, Nickels, and Pennies

Count the money.

Write each amount.

A.

_____ ¢

B.

_____ ¢

C.

_____ ¢

Name_____

Counting with Dimes, Nickels, and Pennies

Count the money.

Write each amount.

A.

_____¢

B.

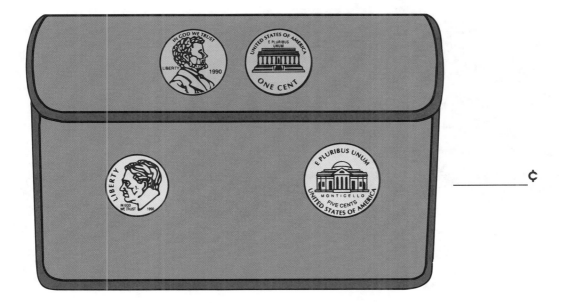

_____¢

Name_____

Counting with Dimes, Nickels, and Pennies

Count the money.

Write each amount.

_____¢

_____¢

Name_____

Counting with Dimes, Nickels, and Pennies

Count the money.

Write each amount.

_____ ¢

_____ ¢

Counting with Dimes, Nickels, and Pennies

Count the money.

Write each amount.

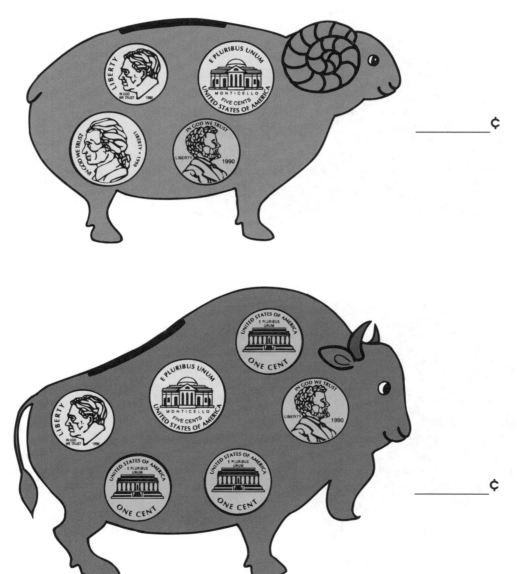

_____ ¢

_____ ¢

Name_____

Counting with Dimes, Nickels, and Pennies

Count the money.

Write each amount.

_____ ¢

_____ ¢

Name_____

Counting with Dimes, Nickels, and Pennies

Count the money.

Write each amount.

_____¢

_____¢

Counting with Dimes, Nickels, and Pennies

Count the money.

Write each amount.

_____¢

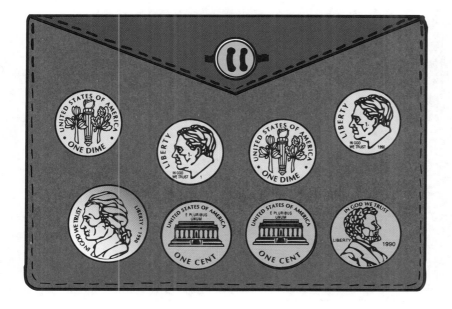

_____¢

Counting with Dimes, Nickels, and Pennies

Count the money.

Write each amount.

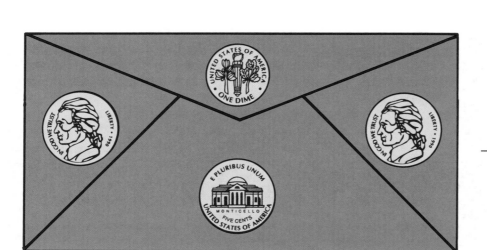

_____ ¢

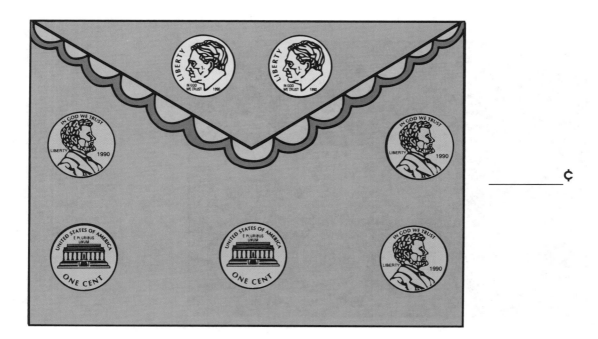

_____ ¢

Counting with Dimes, Nickels, and Pennies

Count the money.

Write each amount.

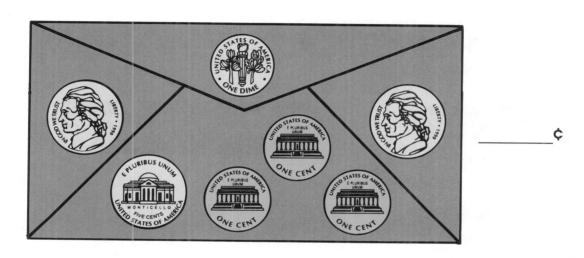

_____¢

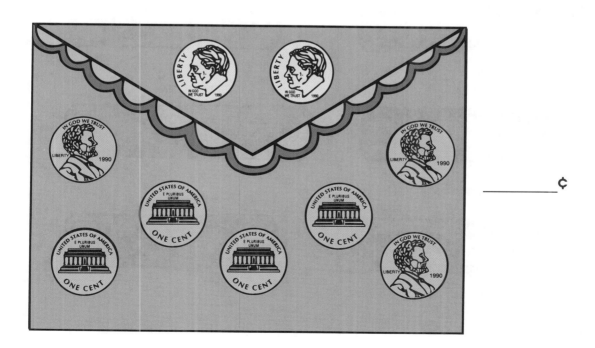

_____¢

Counting with Dimes, Nickels, and Pennies

Count the money on each belt.

Write the amount.

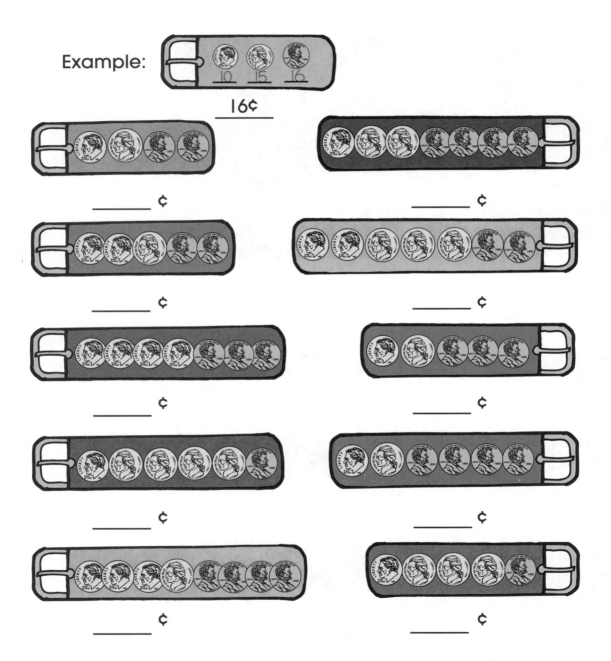

Example:

10 15 16

16¢

_____ ¢   _____ ¢

_____ ¢   _____ ¢

_____ ¢   _____ ¢

_____ ¢   _____ ¢

_____ ¢   _____ ¢

Name_____

Counting with Dimes, Nickels, and Pennies

Circle the block in each set with the greater amount.

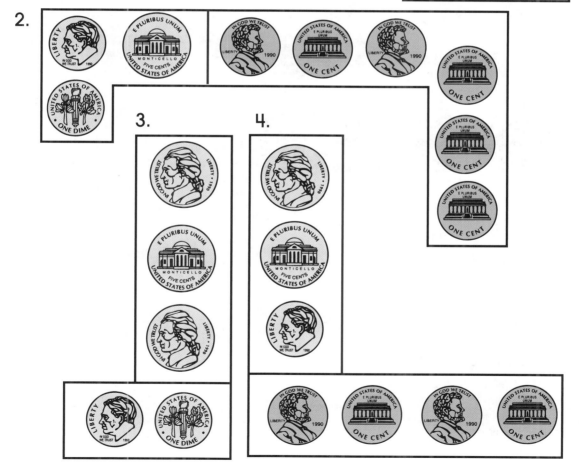

Name_____

Counting with Dimes, Nickels, and Pennies

Count the money.

Write each amount.

1.   _____¢

2.   _____¢

3.

                        _____¢

If you add 1 more penny to
number 1, you will have _____¢

If you add 1 more penny to
number 2, you will have _____¢

If you add 1 more penny to
number 3, you will have _____¢

Counting with Dimes, Nickels, and Pennies

There is a bake sale at school today.

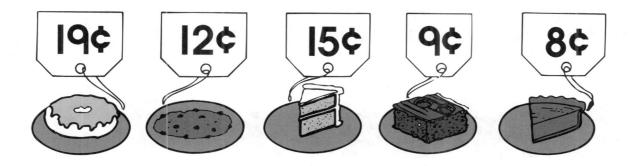

Decide which treat you want.
In the space below, draw enough money to pay for it.

Name_____

Counting with Dimes, Nickels, and Pennies

Answer the questions using the bake sale prices on page 249.

1. Sharita chose the doughnut.
    Circle the money she needed. 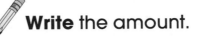 **Write** the amount.

_____ ¢

2. Robert loves brownies.
    Circle the money he needed. **Write** the amount.

_____ ¢

3. Tom had 3 of these.

    He had _____ ¢. He spent it all
    on something good. What does he buy? **Draw** it here.

Name_____

Counting with Dimes, Nickels, and Pennies

Help **Sir Circle count** the coins.
Circle the set with more money.

Example		
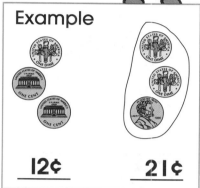		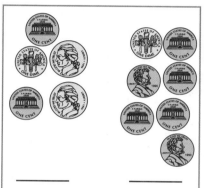

12¢ _____   **21¢** _____

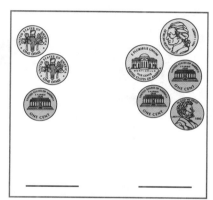

_____   _____

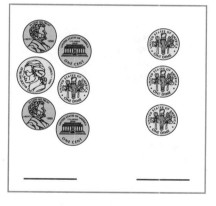

_____   _____

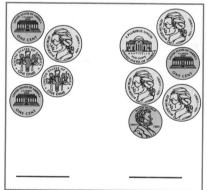

_____   _____

_____   _____

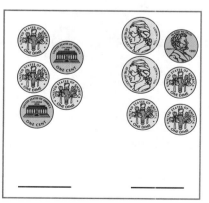

_____   _____

_____   _____

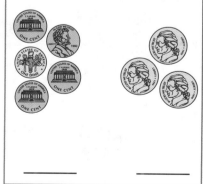

_____   _____

Name_____

Counting with Dimes, Nickels, and Pennies

Count the coins. Use the right color to circle the set of coins with more money.

Example:

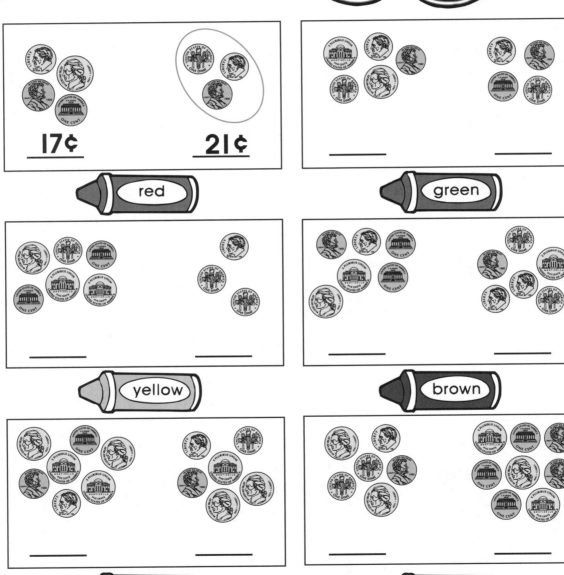

17¢   21¢

red   green

yellow   brown

blue   orange

Name_____

Counting with Dimes, Nickels, and Pennies

Count the money.

Write each amount.

A.

_____¢ _____¢ _____¢ _____¢ _____¢ _____¢

Total

B.

_____¢ _____¢ _____¢ _____¢

_____¢ _____¢ _____¢ _____¢

Total

Name_____

Counting with Dimes, Nickels, and Pennies

Circle the coins that equal the correct amount.

Example:

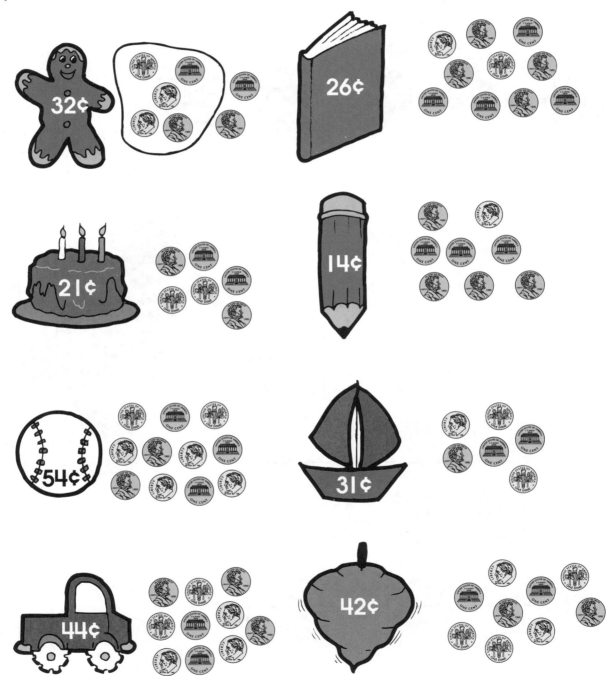

Name_____

Counting with Dimes, Nickels, and Pennies

Circle the coins that equal the correct amount.

Example:

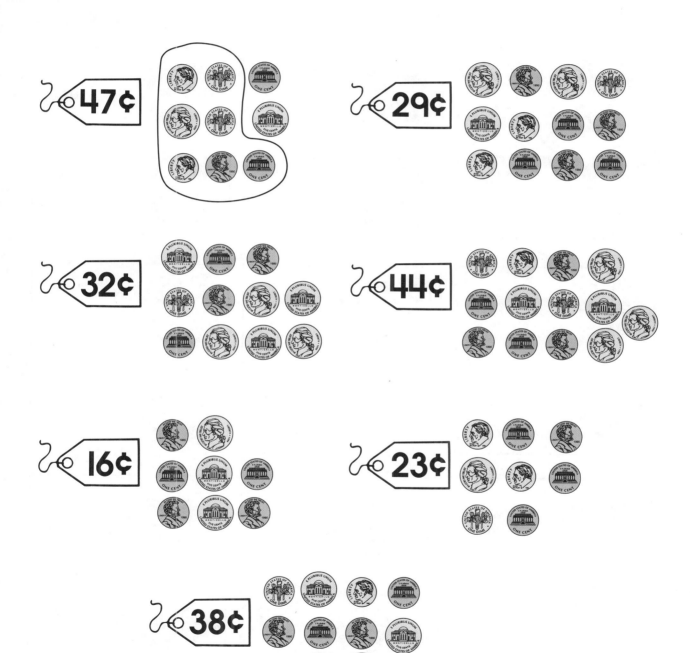

Name_____

Counting with Dimes, Nickels, and Pennies

Draw a line from the coins to the matching amount.

Example:

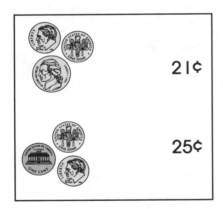
25¢

16¢

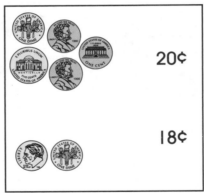
26¢

13¢

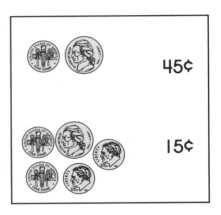
45¢

15¢

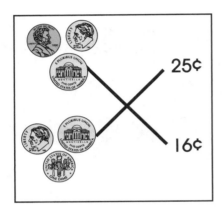
21¢

25¢

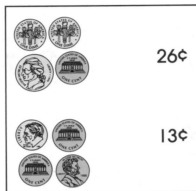
20¢

18¢

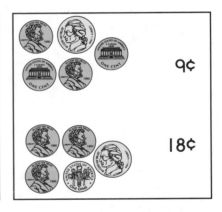
9¢

18¢

15¢

6¢

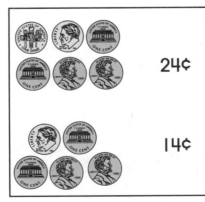
24¢

14¢

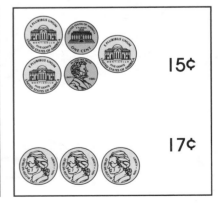
15¢

17¢

Subtracting with Dimes, Nickels, and Pennies

Cross out the coins needed to buy each toy.

Write how much money is left.

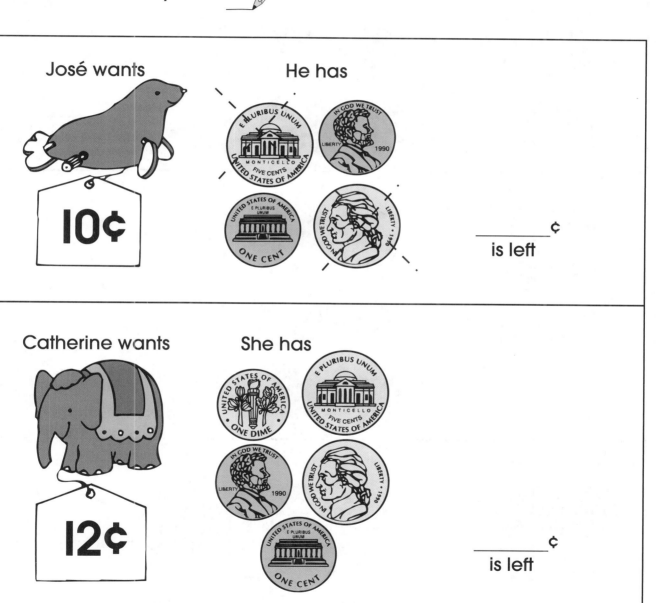

José wants   He has

10¢

_____¢
is left

Catherine wants   She has

12¢

_____¢
is left

Name_____

Subtracting with Dimes, Nickels, and Pennies

Cross out the coins needed to buy each toy. **Write** how much money is left.

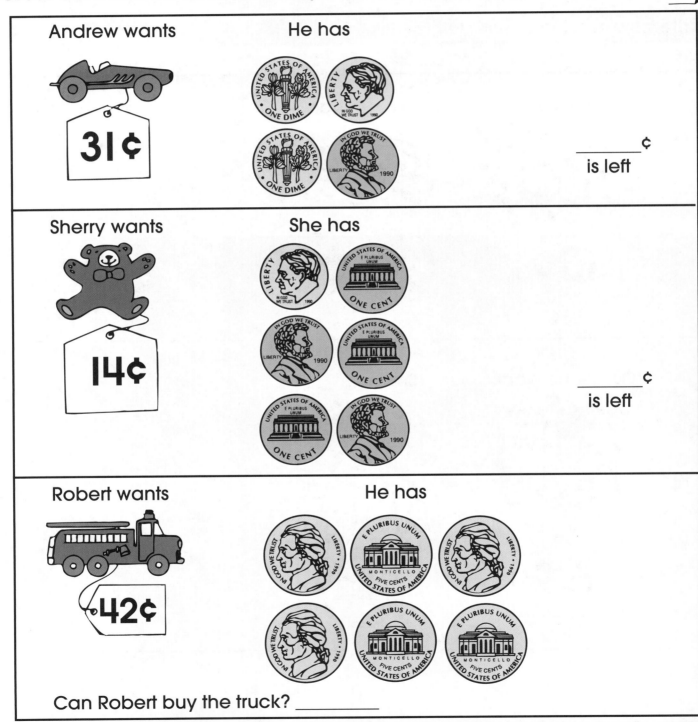

Andrew wants

He has

31¢

_____¢
is left

Sherry wants

She has

14¢

_____¢
is left

Robert wants

He has

42¢

Can Robert buy the truck? _____

Name_____

Subtracting with Dimes, Nickels, and Pennies

Pay the exact amount for each toy. **Cross out** the coins you use.
Write how much money is left.

A.

23¢

Money left: _____ ¢

_____

B.

31¢

Money left: _____¢

_____

C. **Choose** a price between 30¢ and 40¢.
   Write the price on the robot's tag.

¢

Money left: _____ ¢

Name_____

Quarters: Introduction

A quarter is worth 25 cents.
Our first president, **George Washington**, is on the **front**.

Fill in the blanks.

front   back

_____ quarter = _____ pennies

_____ quarter = _____ cents

_____ quarter = _____ ¢

Count these nickels by 5s.

Is this another way to make 25¢?

yes   no

Name_____

Quarters: Introduction

Follow the paths to see how many quarters Mike and Maria can find.

The **bananas** cost **25¢** each.
How many can they buy? _____

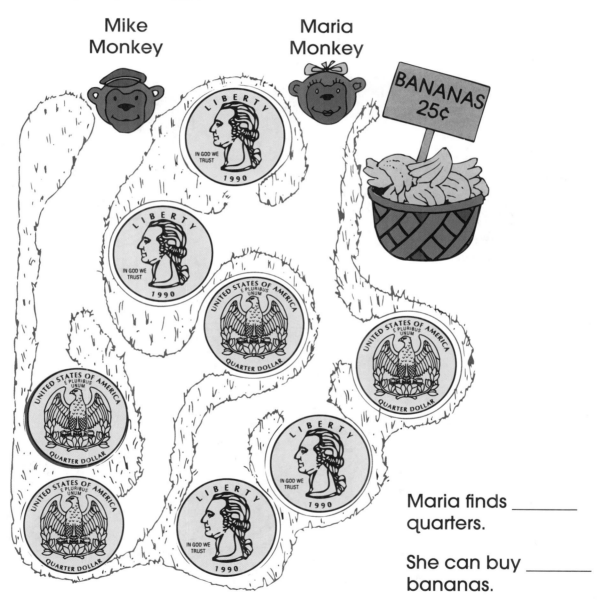

Mike
Monkey

Maria
Monkey

Maria finds _____ quarters.

She can buy _____ bananas.

Mike finds _____ quarters. he can buy _____ bananas.

Name_____

Quarters: Combinations of 25 Cents

These are some ways to make **25¢**.
Color each coin.

 2 dimes,
I nickel

5 nickels

25
pennies

Name_____

Quarters: Combinations of 25 Cents

Count the money.

Write each amount.

A.

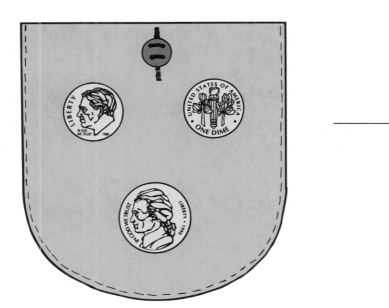

_____ ¢

B.

_____ ¢

Name_____

Quarters: Combinations of 25 Cents

It costs 25¢ to catch a fish.
Circle each group of coins that makes 25¢.

How many fish can I catch?

Draw and **color** the fish I can catch.

Name_____

Quarters: More or Less Than 50 Cents

The tooth fairy left 2 quarters for your shiny baby tooth.

How much money do you have?
Each quarter is worth 25¢.
Two quarters = 50¢

Color each toy you can buy.

Quarters: More Than 25 Cents

Write how much money each boy spent on toy cars.

Terry paid 5¢ for each **blue** car.
Color Terry's cars **blue**.

How much did Terry pay for the **blue** cars?

_____¢

Lucas liked the **red** cars. They were the same price. **Color** his cars **red**

How much did Lucas pay for the **red** cars?

_____¢

Which boy paid more? _____

Name_____

Quarters: 50 Cents or More

Patty bought some pears at the store.
She paid **25¢** for **each pear**. **Color** the pears.

25¢ each

How much money did she spend? _____¢

Jennifer bought some bananas. She paid **10¢** for **each one**.
Color the bananas.

10¢ each

How much money did she spend? _____¢

Which girl spent less? _____

Name_____

Counting with Quarters

These are some machines that use quarters.

Color each machine.

Circle the quarters you need.

Write the number in the blank.

I need _____ quarters to wash clothes.

I need _____ quarter(s) to make a phone call.

Counting with Quarters

Circle the quarters you need.
Color each picture.

Write the number in the blank.

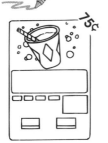   **75¢**

Drinks

I need _____ quarters to buy a drink.

$1.00

I need _____ quarters to buy a comic book.

   **50¢**

I need _____ quarters to buy a frozen fruit bar.

Hurry! It's melting!

Name_____

Counting with Quarters, Dimes, Nickels, and Pennies

Count the money.

Write each amount.

A.

_____ _____ _____ _____

Total

B.

_____ _____ _____ _____ _____

_____ _____

Total

Name_____

Counting with Quarters, Dimes, Nickels, and Pennies

Count the money.

Write each amount.

A.

_____ ¢   _____ ¢   _____ ¢   _____ ¢

Total

B.

_____ ¢   _____ ¢   _____ ¢   _____ ¢

Total

C. **Put** more than 50¢ in the bank. **Show** the coins.

_____ ¢

Total

Name_____

Counting with Quarters, Dimes, Nickels, and Pennies

Count the money. **Write** each amount.

A.

_____ ¢ _____ ¢ _____ ¢ _____ ¢ _____ ¢ _____ ¢

Total

B.

_____ ¢ _____ ¢ _____ ¢ _____ ¢ _____ ¢ _____ ¢

_____ ¢ _____ ¢ _____ ¢

Total

I'm counting my money. 25¢, 35¢, 45¢, 55¢, 60¢, 65¢, 66¢, 67¢.

C. **Solve** this puzzle.
What coins does Lizard have?

Counting with Quarters, Dimes, Nickels, and Pennies

Count the money.

Write each amount.

A.

_____¢

B.

_____¢

Name_____

Counting with Quarters, Dimes, Nickels, and Pennies

Count the money.

Write each amount.

A.

_____¢

B.

_____¢

Name_____

Counting with Quarters, Dimes, Nickels, and Pennies

Draw a line to match each group of coins with the correct amount.

35¢

36¢

40¢

27¢

15¢

21¢

8¢

Name_____

Counting with Quarters, Dimes, Nickels, and Pennies

Count the coins. **Write** the amount in each football.

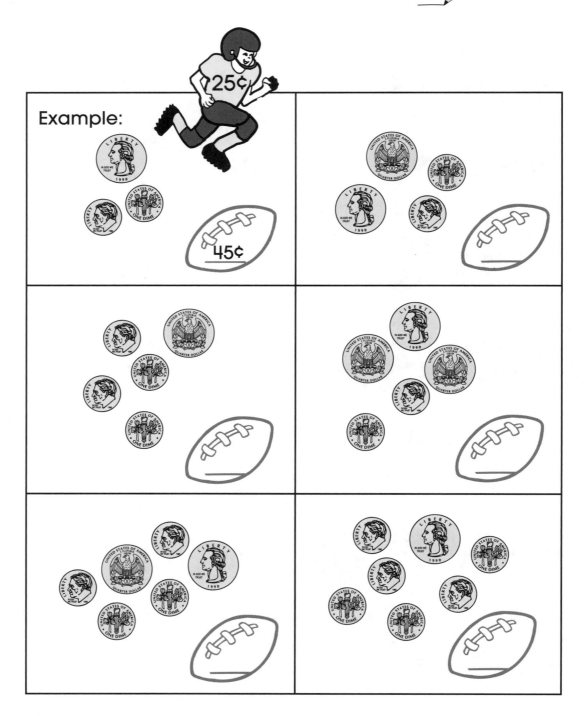

Example:

45¢

Name_____

Counting with Quarters, Dimes, Nickels, and Pennies

Count the coins. **Write** each amount.
Do you have enough money to buy each toy?

Example:	You have...		yes or no
58¢		51¢	no
47¢		_____	_____
75¢		_____	_____
43¢		_____	_____
98¢		_____	_____
32¢		_____	_____
26¢		_____	_____
45¢		_____	_____

Name_____

Counting with Quarters, Dimes, Nickels, and Pennies

(Use with page 279)

Carolyn and Marilyn are going on vacation.

The twins want to buy some things to take along to the beach.
They empty their piggy banks.

Name_____

Counting with Quarters, Dimes, Nickels, and Pennies

(Use with page 278)

Cross out the money Carolyn and Marilyn use to buy 2 pails.

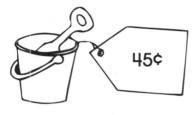

Color the pails pink.

Cross out the money they use to buy 2 beach balls.

 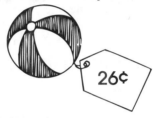

Color the beach balls **red** and yellow.

Cross out the money they use to buy 2 beach towels.

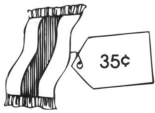 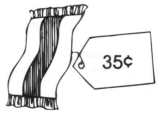

Color the beach towels **blue** and green.

Cross out the money they use to buy 2 pairs of sunglasses.

Color the sunglasses.
Do they have enough money?_____

Name_____

Counting with Quarters, Dimes, Nickels, and Pennies

How many of each coin do you need to buy the items? **Write** the numbers in the boxes.

		Quarters	Dimes	Nickels	Pennies
	(flower band)				
	(brush)				
	(band)				
	(bow)				
	(comb)				

Name_____

Adding and Comparing Amounts of Money

(Use with page 282)

Chris is a good shopper.
He looks for the best prices when he buys school supplies.

Count the money. **Write** each amount. **Circle** and **color** the school supply
Chris bought.

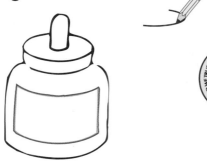

_____¢

or

_____¢

Name_____

Adding and Comparing Amounts of Money

(Use with page 281)

   _____¢

or

      _____¢

_____

   _____¢

or

   _____¢

_____

   **Draw** the coins you think Chris spends for this notebook. Good job, Chris! **Spend wisely!**

How much does he spend? _____¢

Name_____

Adding Quarters, Dimes, Nickels, and Pennies

(Use with page 285)

When Gerald does chores, his mom gives him 7¢ more because he is 7 years old.

Cut and **glue** the extra 7¢ Mom gives Gerald on this page and page 285. **Write** each amount.

Gerald washes the dishes for a quarter. Mom gives him 7¢ extra.

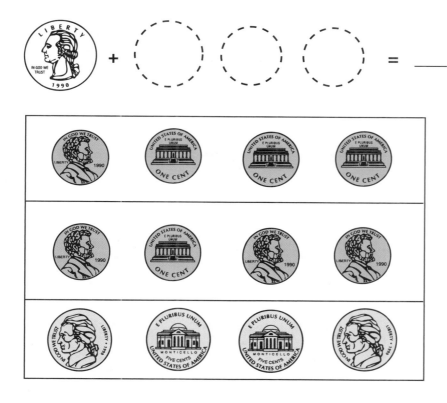

Page is blank for cutting exercise on previous page.

Name_____

Adding Quarters, Dimes, Nickels, and Pennies

(Use with page 283)

Gerald mopped the kitchen floor for 2 dimes, then put wax on it for 2 more dimes.

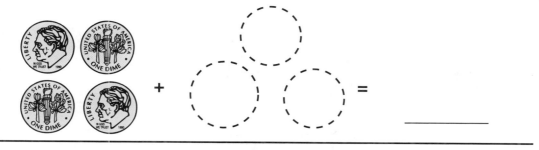

_____

He watered all the plants for 2 nickels.

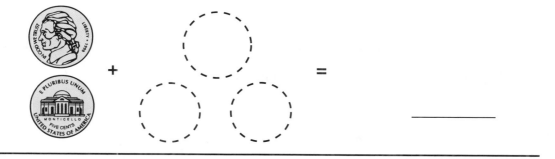

_____

He folded the clothes from the dryer and put them away for 2 dimes, 2 nickels, and 1 penny.

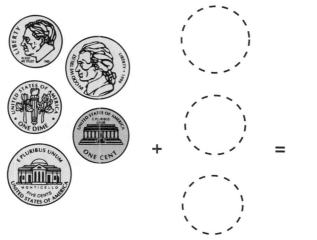

Name_____

Subtracting for Change

Adam wanted to know how much change he would have left when he bought things.

He made this picture to help him subtract.

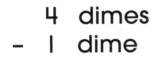

4 dimes
− 1 dime

3 dimes

40¢
− 10¢

30¢

Cross out the dimes. **Solve** the subtraction problem.

6 dimes
− 4 dimes

_____ dimes

60¢
− 40¢

Name_____

Subtracting for Change

Pay the exact amount for each toy.
Cross out the coins you use. **Write** how much money is left.

Money left: _____ ¢

Money left: _____ ¢

Money left: _____ ¢

Name_____

Subtracting for Change

Cross out the coins Adam uses to buy each toy.
Write each subtraction problem.
Example:

Name_____

Subtracting from 50 Cents

Maria went to the store to buy a birthday gift for her best friend.

Maria took 50¢ to the store.

Circle each thing Maria can buy.

Name_____

Subtracting from 50 Cents

Maria wanted to know how much change she would get back from each toy. **Subtract**. **Write** how much money is left.

50¢
–   ¢
_____

50¢
–   ¢
_____

50¢
–   ¢
_____

50¢
–   ¢
_____

Making Exact Amounts of Money

Pay the exact amount for each toy. Use as few dimes, nickels, and pennies as you can.

A.　What coins did you use to buy the bug?

_____ dimes _____ nickels

_____ pennies

B.　What coins did you use to buy the spider?

_____ dimes _____ nickels

_____ pennies

C.　What coins did Cat use to pay for the ball?

_____ dimes _____ nickels

_____ pennies

Name_____

Making Exact Amounts of Money

Use as few dimes, nickels and pennies as you can.
Pay the exact amount for each toy.

A. What coins did you use to buy the turtle?

_____ dimes _____ nickels

_____ penny

B. What coins did you use to buy the snail?

_____ dimes

_____ nickel _____ pennies

C. What coins did Alligator use
to pay for the toothbrush?

_____ dime _____ nickels

_____ pennies

I used three coins to pay.

Name_____

Making Exact Amounts of Money

Use as few quarters, dimes, nickels and pennies as you can.
Pay the exact amount for each toy.

A. What coins did you use to buy the bee?

_____ quarter _____ dimes

_____ nickels _____pennies

B. What coins did you use to buy the bicycle?

_____ quarter _____ dime

_____ nickel _____ pennies

C. What coins did Bird use
to pay for the pilot wings?

_____ quarters _____ dimes

_____ nickels _____ pennies

Name_____

Making Exact Amounts of Money

Use as few quarters, dimes, nickels and pennies as you can.
Pay the exact amount for each toy.

A. What coins did you use to buy the bug?

_____ quarters _____ dimes

_____ nickels _____ pennies

B. What coins did you use to buy the skates?

_____ quarter _____ dimes

_____ nickels _____ pennies

C. What coins did Frog use
to pay for the bow tie?

_____ quarters _____ dimes

_____ nickels _____ pennies

Name_____

Making Exact Amounts of Money

Use as few quarters, dimes, nickels and pennies as you can.
Pay the exact amount for each toy.

A. What coins did you use to buy the ring?

_____ quarters _____ dime

_____ nickel _____ penny

B. What coins did you use to buy the foot?

_____ quarters _____ dimes

_____ nickels _____ pennies

C. What coins did Rabbit
use to pay for the watch?

_____ quarters _____ dimes

_____ nickels _____ pennies

Name_____

Making Exact Amounts of Money and Change

Pay the exact amount for each toy.
Cross out the coins you use. **Write** how much money is left.

Money left: _____¢

Money left: _____¢

Choose a price between 42¢ and 58¢. **Write** the price on the tag.

Money left: _____¢

Name_____

Making Exact Amounts of Money and Change

Pay the exact amount for each toy.
Cross out the coins you use. **Write** how much money is left.

Money left: _____ ¢

Money left: _____ ¢

How much money does Turtle have left after buying the balloon?

I had 2 dimes, 2 nickels and 2 pennies. Now I have one coin left.

Money left: _____ ¢

Name_____

Making Exact Amounts of Money and Change

Pay the exact amount for each toy.
Cross out the coins you use. **Write** how much money is left.

Money left: _____ ¢

_____

Money left: _____ ¢

_____

How much money does Squirrel have left
after buying the sunglasses?

60¢

I had 2 quarters, 3
dimes and 1 nickel.
I paid for the
sunglasses. Now I
have one coin left.

Money left: _____ ¢

Name_____

Problem Solving with Money

To be a good problem solver, you must **read the problem carefully**.

Think: What do I want to know? _____

plant **26¢**

frog **15¢**

car **14¢**

ball **7¢**

ring **8¢**

horn **9¢**

Solve each problem.

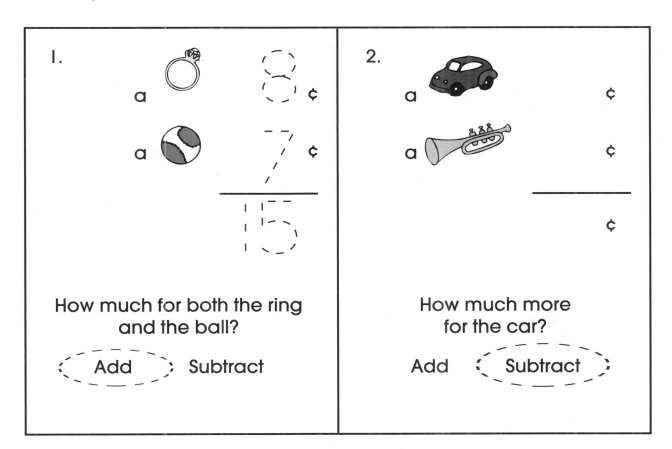

1.
a ⭕ _____ ¢

a ⚾ _____ ¢

_____
15

How much for both the ring
and the ball?

(**Add**) Subtract

2.
a 🚗 _____ ¢

a 🎺 _____ ¢

_____

_____ ¢

How much more
for the car?

Add (**Subtract**)

Problem Solving with Money

(Use with page 299)

---

3. a _____ ¢

    a _____ ¢

How much more for
the plant?
Add   Subtract

---

4. a _____ ¢

    a _____ ¢

How much for both the
horn and the ring?
Add   Subtract

---

5. a _____ ¢

    a _____ ¢

How much for both
the ball and car?
Add   Subtract

---

6. a _____ ¢

    a _____ ¢

How much more
for the frog?
Add   Subtract

---

7. **Circle** the one that
costs more.

---

8. **Circle** the one that
costs more.

Buy a , a and a .

How much for all three?

_____ ¢ + _____ ¢ + _____ ¢ = _____ ¢

Name_____

Problem Solving with Money

Draw the coins you use to buy each item.
Write the number of coins on each blank. Use as few coins as you can.

9¢

_____ dimes

_____ nickels

_____ pennies

11¢

_____ dime

_____ nickels

_____ penny

14¢

_____ dime

_____ nickels

_____ pennies

Find another way to pay for this.

14¢

_____ dimes

_____ nickels

_____ pennies

Name_____

Problem Solving with Money

Draw the coins you use to buy each item.
Write the number of coins on each blank. Use as few coins as you can.

13¢

_____ dime

_____ nickels

_____ pennies

15¢

_____ dime

_____ nickel

_____ pennies

18¢

_____ dime

_____ nickel

_____ pennies

Find another way
to pay for this.

18¢

_____ dimes

_____ nickels

_____ pennies

Name_____

Problem Solving with Money

Draw the coins you use to buy each item.
Write the number of coins on each blank. Use as few coins as you can.

  35¢

_____ quarter

_____ dime

_____ nickels

_____ pennies

  29¢

_____ quarter

_____ dimes

_____ nickels

_____ pennies

 43¢

_____ quarter

_____ dime

_____ nickel

_____ pennies

Find another way
to pay for this.

 43¢

_____ quarters

_____ dimes

_____ nickels

_____ pennies

Problem Solving with Money

Draw the coins you use to buy each item.
Write the number of coins on each blank. Use as few coins as you can.

50¢	66¢
_____ quarters	_____ quarters
_____ dimes	_____ dime
_____ nickels	_____ nickel
_____ pennies	_____ penny
70¢	**Find another way to pay for this.** 70¢
_____ quarters	_____ quarter
_____ dimes	_____ dimes
_____ nickels	_____ nickel
_____ pennies	_____ pennies

Name_____

Making Exact Amounts of Money: Two Ways to Pay

Find two ways to pay. Use as few coins as you can.
Write what coins you use.

27¢

_____ quarter   _____ quarters

_____ dimes   _____ dimes

_____ nickels   _____ nickel

_____ pennies   _____ pennies

32¢

_____ quarter   _____ quarters

_____ dimes   _____ dimes

_____ nickel   _____ nickels

_____ pennies   _____ pennies

Name_____

Making Exact Amounts of Money: Two Ways to Pay

Find two ways to pay. Use as few coins as you can.
Write what coins you use.

_____ quarter   _____ quarters

_____ dime   _____ dimes

_____ nickels   _____ nickels

_____ pennies   _____ pennies

_____ quarter   _____ quarters

_____ dime   _____ dimes

_____ nickel   _____ nickels

_____ pennies   _____ pennies

Making Exact Amounts of Money: Two Ways to Pay

Find two ways to pay. Use as few coins as you can.
Write what coins you use.

_____ quarters   _____ quarters

_____ dimes   _____ dimes

_____ nickels   _____ nickels

_____ pennies   _____ pennies

_____ quarters   _____ quarters

_____ dime   _____ dimes

_____ nickel   _____ nickel

_____ pennies   _____ pennies

Making Exact Amounts of Money: How Much More?

Count the money.
Write how much more money you need to pay the exact amount.

How much money do you have? _____ ¢

How much more money do you need? _____ ¢

_____

How much money do you have? _____ ¢

How much more money do you need? _____ ¢

_____

How much money does Frog have? _____ ¢

How much more money does
Frog need?

_____ ¢

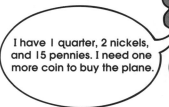

I have 1 quarter, 2 nickels, and 15 pennies. I need one more coin to buy the plane.

Name_____

Making Exact Amounts of Money: How Much More?

Count the money.
Write how much more money you need to pay the exact amount.

How much money do you have? _____ ¢

How much more money do you need? _____ ¢

_____

How much money do you have? _____ ¢

How much more money do you need? _____ ¢

_____

How much money does
Monkey have?

_____ ¢

How much more money does
Monkey need?

_____ ¢

Name_____

Half Dollars: Introduction

Look at each side of the half dollar.

Color both sides silver.

front   back

The half dollar is worth 50¢.

Fill in the blanks.

_____ half dollar = _____ pennies

_____ half dollar = _____ cents

_____ half dollar = _____ ¢

Half Dollars: Introduction

These are some ways to make 50¢:

Color each coin.

1 half dollar

2 quarters

10 nickels

5 dimes

50 pennies

Name_____

Counting Half Dollars, Quarters, Dimes, Nickels, and Pennies

Count the money.
Write each amount.

_____ ¢   _____ ¢   _____ ¢   _____ ¢
                                                            Total

_____

_____ ¢   _____ ¢   _____ ¢   _____ ¢   _____ ¢
                                                     Total

_____

Draw between 50¢ and 90¢ in the jar.

Name_____

Counting Half Dollars, Quarters, Dimes, Nickels, and Pennies

Count the money.
Write each amount.

_____ ¢   _____ ¢   _____ ¢   _____ ¢

_____ Total

___ ¢   ___ ¢   ___ ¢   ___ ¢   ___ ¢   _____ ¢

_____ Total

Draw more than 80¢ in the pocket.

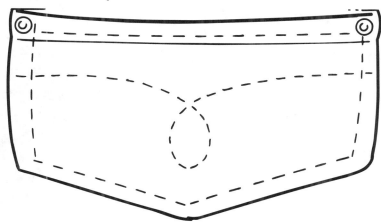

Name_____

Counting Coins: How Much More?

Count the money.
Write how much more money you need to pay the exact amount.

How much money do you have? _____ ¢

How much more money do you need? _____ ¢

_____

How much money do you have? _____ ¢

How much more money do you need? _____ ¢

_____

How much money does Alligator have? _____ ¢

How much more money does Alligator need?

_____ ¢

Name_____

Counting Coins: How Much More?

Count the money.
Write how much more money you need to pay the exact amount.

How much money do you have? _____ ¢

How much more money do you need? _____ ¢

_____

How much money do you have? _____ ¢

How much more money do you need? _____ ¢

_____

How much money does Raccoon have? _____ ¢

How much more money does Raccoon need?

_____ ¢

I have 1 half-dollar, 1 quarter, 2 dimes, 1 nickel and 4 pennies. I need one more coin to buy the spyglass.

Name_____

Dollar Bills: Introduction

This is a **dollar bill**.

It has **2 sides**.

Color them green.

Fill in the blanks.

1 dollar = $1.00

1 dollar = __one dollar__

1 dollar = __100__ pennies

1 dollar = __100__ ¢

Dollar Bills: Introduction

This is the **dollar sign**: **$**
It is an S with a line through it.

Trace the dollar signs.

There is a period between
the dollars and the cents: $1.00

Name_____

Dollar Bills: Introduction

There are many ways to make one dollar.

1 dollar bill

2 half dollars

4 quarters

100 pennies

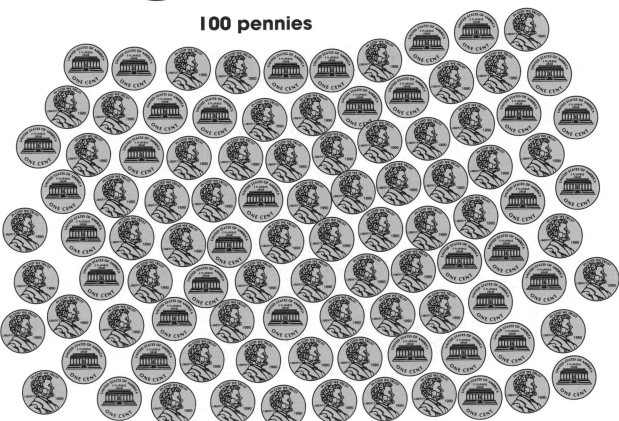

Dollar Bills: Introduction

Count each set of coins.
If the coins equal 100 cents, **write** $1.00 on the line.

Count by 10s with dimes. _____

Count by 5s with nickels. _____

Name_____

Counting with Dollar Bills and Coins

Writing Dollar Amounts

Here are tips for writing dollar amounts:
1. Drop the ¢ sign.
2. Add the $ sign.
3. Use a . (period) between the dollars and cents.

Write each amount of dollars and cents.

1.

$ 1.08

2.

$ _____._____

Name_____

Counting with Dollar Bills and Coins

A one-dollar bill is worth 100¢ or $1.00.

Count the money.
Write each amount.

A.

$ _____ $ _____ $ _125_
                                              Total

B.

$ _____ $ _____ $ _____ $ _____
                                              Total

C. Draw about $2.00 in the bank. Use a one-dollar bill.

Name_____

Counting with Dollar Bills and Coins

Count the money.
Write each amount.

1.  $_____._____

2.   $ _____._____

3.  $ _____._____

4.  $ _____._____

Matching Dollar Amounts

Count the money.
Draw a line to match each group of dollar bills and coins to the correct amount.

$1.07

$1.37

$1.32

$1.12

Name_____

Matching Dollar Amounts

Count the money.
Draw a line to match each group of dollar bills and coins to the correct amount.

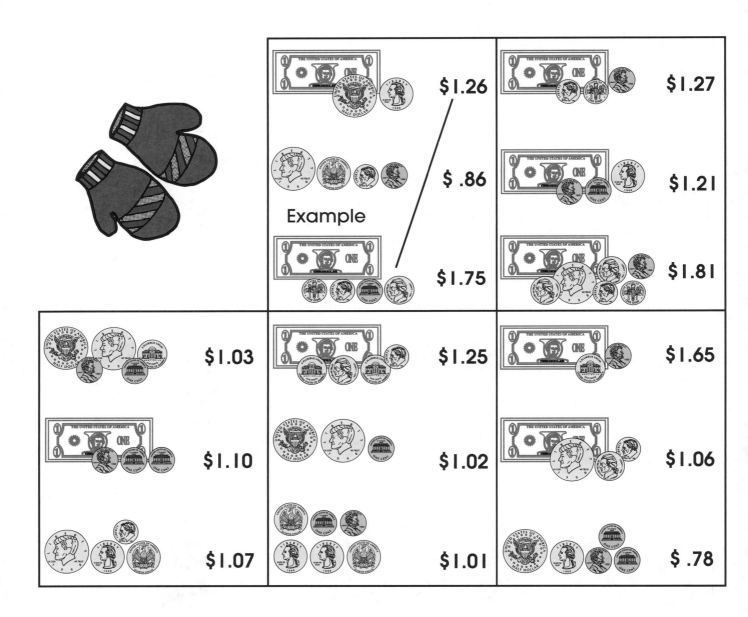

$1.26

$ .86

Example

$1.75

$1.27

$1.21

$1.81

$1.03

$1.10

$1.07

$1.25

$1.02

$1.01

$1.65

$1.06

$ .78

Name_____

Counting Dollar Bills and Coins: How Much More?

Count the coins and bills.
Write how much more money you need to pay the exact amount.

A.

How much money do you have? $ _____

How much more money do you need? _____¢

B.

How much money do you have? $ _____

How much more money do you need? _____¢

C. How much more money does Anteater have?

$ _____

How much more money does Anteater need?

_____¢

I have 1 dollar bill, 1 quarter, 1 dime and 1 penny. I need one more coin to buy the flashlight.

$1.61

Estimating Amounts of Money

Round up or down to make an estimate about money.

Circle the amount that is closer to the amount on the tag.
This is an estimate.

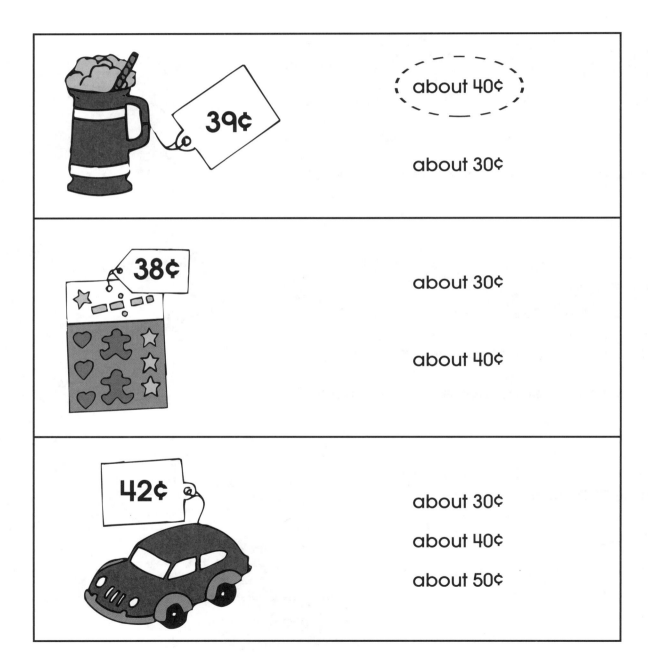

39¢

about 40¢

about 30¢

38¢

about 30¢

about 40¢

42¢

about 30¢

about 40¢

about 50¢

Name_____

Estimating Amounts of Money

Circle the closest estimate.

 $1.49

about 50¢

about $1.40

about $1.50

 **$2.98**

about $2.00

about $3.00

about $4.00

 **$1.98**

about $1.00

about $2.00

about $3.00

 **$3.05**

about $2.00

about $3.00

about $4.00

Name_____

Adding and Subtracting
Amounts of Money: Using Estimation

(Use with page 329.)

Using estimation makes it much easier to add or subtract in your head. These foods are for sale in the lunchroom.

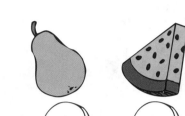

39¢   21¢   19¢   11¢   29¢

You have this much money:

  You have _____ cents.

You want the . **Estimate** the cost. _____ ¢

Do you have enough money? _____

The and look good.

Add the estimated prices.

You probably have enough money!

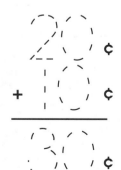

Name_____

Adding and Subtracting Amounts of Money: Using Estimation

You have this much money:

You have _____ cents.

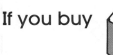

If you buy [milk], will you have enough money left to buy a ? _____

money you have =   _____ ¢

estimated milk =   - _____ ¢

_____ ¢

You have this much money:

You have _____ cents.

You want to buy and an .   _____ ¢

+ _____ ¢

Add the estimated prices

_____ ¢

Do you have enough money? _____

Which other fruit can you buy with your milk? _____

Name_____

Adding and Subtracting Amounts of Money: Making Change

How much change should you get?

Example:

I buy:

29¢
+ 14¢
____
43¢

I have:

55¢
- 43¢
____

Change 12¢

I buy:

56¢
+ 27¢
____

I have:

Change ☐

I buy:

$0.61
+ 0.59
____

I have:

$0.50

Change ☐

I buy:

$0.78
+$0.69
____

I have:

Change ☐

I buy:

$0.59
+ $0.86
____

I have:

Change ☐

I buy:

$0.66
+ $0.75
____

I have:

Change ☐

Name_____

Adding and Subtracting
Amounts of Money: Making Change

How much change should you get?

Example:

Lunch:	I have:
59¢	$1.15
17¢	− 0.76
76¢	Change **39¢**

Lunch:	I have:
$0.86	
+ $0.15	
	Change

Lunch:	I have:
$0.75	
+ $0.16	
	Change

Lunch:	I have:
$0.66	
+ $1.26	
	Change

Lunch:	I have:
$0.77	
$0.54	
	Change

Lunch:	I have:
$0.64	
+ $0.89	
	Change

Name_____

Making Change: Money Puzzles

Solve each puzzle.
Write how much change you will get.

A. Use 2 quarters.

How much change will you get?

_____

B. Use 1 quarter, 2 dimes and 2 nickels.

How much change will you get?

_____

C. Use 3 quarters and 1 dime.

How much change will you get?

_____

D. Use 3 quarters and 2 nickels.

How much change will you get?

_____

Name_____

Making Change: Money Puzzles

Solve each puzzle.
Write how much change you will get.

A. Use 1 one-dollar bill.

How much change will you get?

_____

B. Use 1 half-dollar and 2 quarters.

How much change will you get?

_____

C. Use 1 one-dollar bill and 1 quarter.

How much change will you get?

_____

D. Use 2 half-dollars, 1 quarter and 1 dime.

How much change will you get?

_____

Name_____

Making Change: Money Puzzles

Solve each puzzle.
Write how much change you will get.

A. Use 3 half-dollars.

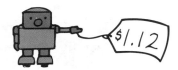

$1.12

How much change will you get?

_____

B. Use 1 one-dollar bill,
2 quarters and 1 dime.

$1.54

How much change will you get?

_____

C. Use 1 one-dollar bill,
1 half-dollar and 1 quarter.

$1.68

How much change will you get?

_____

D. Use 1 one-dollar bill and
2 half-dollars.

$1.51

How much change will you get?

_____

Name_____

Making Change: Money Puzzles

Solve each puzzle.
Write how much change you will get.

A.   Use 2 one-dollar bills.

$1.59

How much change will you get?

_____

B.   Use 2 one-dollar bills.

$1.85

How much change will you get?

_____

C.   Use 3 one-dollar bills.

$2.65

How much change will you get?

_____

D.   Use 3 one-dollar bills.

$2.06

How much change will you get?

_____

Making Change: Money Puzzles

Solve each puzzle.
Write how much change you will get.

A. Use 4 one-dollar bills.

How much change will you get?

_____

B. Use 5 one-dollar bills.

How much change will you get?

_____

C. Use 3 one-dollar bills.

How much change will you get?

_____

D. Use 2 one-dollar bills.

How much change will you get?

_____

Name_____

Making Exact Amounts of Money

Pay for each toy. Use as few coins as you can.
Write what coins you use.

A.

_____ quarters

_____ dime

_____ nickels

B.

_____ quarters

_____ dimes

_____ nickel

C.

_____ quarters

_____ dimes

_____ nickel

Name_____

Making Exact Amounts of Money

Pay for each snack. Use as few coins as you can.
Write what coins you use.

A.

_____ quarters
_____ dime
_____ nickel
_____ pennies

B.

_____ quarter
_____ dimes
_____ nickels
_____ pennies

C.

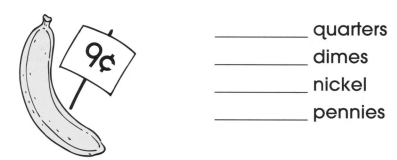

_____ quarters
_____ dimes
_____ nickel
_____ pennies

Making Exact Amounts of Money

Pay for each toy. Use as few coins as you can.
Write what coins you use.

A.

85¢

_____ half-dollar

_____ quarter

_____ dime

_____ nickels

_____ pennies

B.

$1.00

_____ half-dollars

_____ quarters

_____ dimes

_____ nickels

_____ pennies

C.

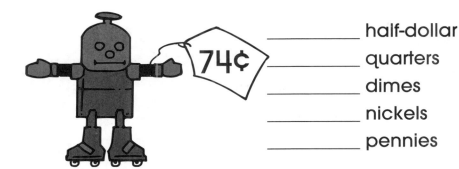

74¢

_____ half-dollar

_____ quarters

_____ dimes

_____ nickels

_____ pennies

Name_____

Making Exact Amounts of Money

Pay for each toy. Use as few coins as you can.
Write what coins you use.

A.

_____ half-dollars
_____ quarters
_____ dimes
_____ nickels
_____ pennies

B.

_____ half-dollars
_____ quarter
_____ dime
_____ nickels
_____ pennies

C.

_____ half-dollar
_____ quarter
_____ dimes
_____ nickels
_____ pennies

Name_____

Making Exact Amounts of Money

Pay for each toy. Use as few coins as you can.
Write what coins you use.

A.

$1.30

_____ dollar

_____ half-dollars

_____ quarter

_____ dimes

_____ nickel

_____ pennies

B.

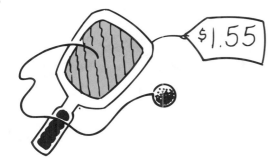

$1.55

_____ dollar

_____ half-dollar

_____ quarters

_____ dimes

_____ nickel

_____ pennies

C.

$1.64

_____ dollar

_____ half-dollar

_____ quarters

_____ dime

_____ nickels

_____ pennies

Making Exact Amounts of Money

Pay for each toy. Use as few coins as you can.
Write what coins you use.

A.

$1.05

_____ dollar

_____ half-dollars

_____ quarters

_____ dimes

_____ nickel

_____ pennies

B.

$1.75

_____ dollar

_____ half-dollar

_____ quarter

_____ dimes

_____ nickels

_____ pennies

C.

$1.39

_____ dollar

_____ half-dollars

_____ quarter

_____ dime

_____ nickels

_____ pennies

Name_____

Using Combinations of Coins to Pay

Pay for each dessert.
Use as few coins as you can.

	![quarter]	![dime]	![nickel]	![penny]	Number of Coins Used
A. 28¢	1			3	4
B. 39¢					
C. 49¢					
D. 56¢					

Name_____

Using Combinations of Coins to Pay

Pay for each toy.
Use as few coins as you can.

					Number of Coins Used
A. 22¢					
B. 37¢					
C. 52¢					
D. 97¢					

Using Combinations of Coins to Pay

Pay for each book.
Use as few coins as you can.

					Number of Coins Used
A. SUPER 75¢					
B. SPORT 80¢					
C. Monster 97¢					
D. MAGIC 66¢					

Name_____

Using Combinations of Coins to Pay

Pay for each snack.
Use as few coins as you can.

					Number of Coins Used
A. $1.05					
B. 95¢					
C. 85¢					
D. 65¢					

Name_____

Using Combinations of Coins to Pay

Pay for each mask.
Use as few coins and bills as you can.

					Number of Coins Used
A. $1.75					
B. $1.95					
C. $2.50					
D. $3.15					

Name_____

Making Exact Amounts
of Money Two Ways

Write two ways to pay for each thing.
Pay the exact amount.

A.

40¢

	Dimes	Nickels	Pennies
Way 1	4		
Way 2		8	

B.

34¢

	Dimes	Nickels	Pennies
Way 1			
Way 2			

C.

61¢

	Dimes	Nickels	Pennies
Way 1			
Way 2			

Name_____

Making Exact Amounts
of Money Two Ways

Write two ways to pay for each thing.
Pay the exact amount.

A.

	Quarters	Dimes	Nickels	Pennies
Way 1				
Way 2				

B.

	Quarters	Dimes	Nickels	Pennies
Way 1				
Way 2				

C.

	Quarters	Dimes	Nickels	Pennies
Way 1				
Way 2				

Name_____

Making Exact Amounts
of Money Two Ways

Write two ways to pay for each thing.
Pay the exact amount.

STICK-ON JEWELS $1.25

A.

	Half Dollars	Quarters	Dimes	Nickels	Pennies
Way 1					
Way 2					

B.

$1.50

	Half Dollars	Quarters	Dimes	Nickels	Pennies
Way 1					
Way 2					

$1.17

C.

	Half Dollars	Quarters	Dimes	Nickels	Pennies
Way 1					
Way 2					

Making Exact Amounts of Money Two Ways

Write two ways to pay for each thing.
Pay the exact amount.

A.

	$1 Bills	Half Dollars	Quarters	Dimes	Nickels
Way 1					
Way 2					

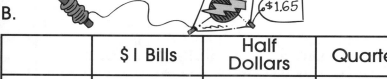

B.

	$1 Bills	Half Dollars	Quarters	Dimes	Nickels
Way 1					
Way 2					

C. **Solve** this puzzle.
What's missing in each way to pay?

	$1 Bills	Half Dollars	Quarters	Dimes	Nickels
Way 1	2			2	
Way 2		4	1		

Making Exact Amounts of Money Two Ways

Write two ways to pay for each thing.
Pay the exact amount.

$5.60

A.

	$1 Bills	Half Dollars	Quarters	Dimes	Nickels	Pennies
Way 1						
Way 2						

$5.95 JUMBO MARKERS

B.

	$1 Bills	Half Dollars	Quarters	Dimes	Nickels	Pennies
Way 1						
Way 2						

C.

$6.72

Solve this puzzle.
What's missing in each way to pay?

	$1 Bills	Half Dollars	Quarters	Dimes	Nickels	Pennies
Way 1	5	1				12
Way 2	4		1			7

Estimating Amounts of Money

banana	pudding	popcorn	cookies	crackers & peanut butter
10¢	25¢	30¢	20¢	15¢

Use the coins.
If you spend all your money, which snacks can you buy?
First, estimate. **Then**, check.

A.

I can buy:_____

B.

I can buy:_____

C. **Solve** the puzzle.
Ahmad had 1 quarter, 2 dimes, 1 nickel
and 10 pennies. He bought two snacks.
He has less than 10 cents left.

What snacks did he buy? _____

Name_____

Estimating Amounts of Money

25¢   65¢   50¢   55¢   70¢   35¢

Use the coins.
If you spend all your money, which pet treats
can you buy? **First**, estimate. **Then**, check.

A.

I can buy:_____

B.

I can buy:_____

C. **Solve** the puzzle.
   Ismelda had 3 quarters. She bought a pet treat.
   She has 2 quarters left.

   What treat did she buy? _____

Name_____

Estimating Amounts of Money

Use the coins and bills.
If you spend all your money, what tickets can you buy?
First, estimate. **Then**, check.

A.

I can buy:_____

B.

I can buy:_____

C. **Solve** the puzzle.
Larry and Leticia had 3 half-dollars. They bought 2 different tickets. They used all of their money.

What tickets did they buy? _____

Estimating Amounts of Money

Kassie's Cafe

Hamburger........90¢

Cheeseburger...$1.00

Burrito...............$1.00

Small Pizza........75¢

Super Salad......80¢

Milk....................35¢

Chocolate Milk...45¢

Apple Juice........55¢

Berry Juice..........65¢

Dream Bar..........75¢

Use the coins and bills. Choose one main dish and one drink or dessert. If you spend all your money, what can you buy? **First**, estimate. **Then**, check.

A.

I can buy:_____

B.

I can buy:_____

C. **Solve** the puzzle.
Tina had 2 half-dollars, 1 dime, and 2 nickels. She bought one food and one drink. She has 10 cents left.

What did Tina buy?_____

Estimating Amounts of Money

Whale of a Sale - Birthday Gifts

| eraser $1.00 | pen $1.10 | patch $0.75 | keyring $0.85 | button $1.25 | cards $1.20 | jug $1.50 |

Use the coins and bills.
If you spend all your money, what can you buy?
First, estimate. **Then**, check.

A.

I can buy: _____

B.

I can buy:_____

C. **Solve** the puzzle.
Martin had 2 one-dollar bills.
He bought one gift. He has less than $1.00 left.

Which of the gifts could Martin have bought?

_____

Making Change

Pay the exact amount.
Write how much change you will get back.

A.

Amount you get back:

_____ ¢

B.

Amount you get back:

_____ ¢

C.

Amount you get back:

_____ ¢

Making Change

Pay the exact amount.
Write how much change you will get back.

A.

Amount you get back:

_____ ¢

B.

Amount you get back:

_____ ¢

C.

Amount you get back:

_____ ¢

Name_____

Making Change

Pay the exact amount.
Write how much change you will get back.

A.

Amount you get back:

_____¢

B.

Amount you get back:

_____¢

C.

Amount you get back:

_____¢

Making Change

Pay the exact amount.
Write how much change you will get back.

A.

Amount you get back: _____ ¢

B.

Amount you get back: _____ ¢

C. **Solve** the puzzle.

How much does Abby pay?
Write the amount on the tag.

I had 2 one-dollar bills.
I paid for the kite. I got
back a quarter, 1 dime
and 1 penny.

Making Change

Pay the exact amount.
Write how much change you will get back.

A.

$2.34

Amount you get back: _____ ¢

B.

$2.75

Amount you get back: $_____

C. Solve the puzzle.

How much does Dominic pay?
Write the amount on the tag.

I had five one-dollar bills. I paid for the compass. I got back 2 one-dollar bills, 1 quarter and 3 pennies.

Name_____

Money Puzzles

Solve each puzzle.
Draw the coins.

A. There are 4 identical coins in the bag. Together they are worth more than 35¢, but less than 50¢. What coins could they be?

B. There are 4 coins in the bag. Two are worth more than 25¢ each. Two are worth less than 10¢ each. What could they be?

C. There are 5 coins in the bag. Together they are worth more than 90¢. What coins could they be?

D. There are 6 coins in the bag. Together they are worth between 75¢ and $1.00. What coins could they be?

Money Puzzles

Solve each puzzle.
Draw the coins.

A. There are 5 coins in the bank. Together they are worth $1.00 exactly. What coins could they be?

B. There are 4 coins in the bank. Together they are worth exactly 80¢. What coins could they be?

C. There are 6 coins in the bank. Two are worth more than 10¢ each. Four are worth less than 10¢ each. All together they are worth more than $1.15. What coins could they be?

D. There are 6 coins in the bank. Four are worth more than 10¢ each. Two are worth less than 25¢ each. All together they are worth $1.20. What coins could they be?

Name_____

Using Combinations of Coins to Pay

Use the coins shown to make each amount.

A. Use 3 coins to make 25¢.			2	1	
B. Use 4 coins to make 50¢.					
C. Use 4 coins to make 66¢.					
D. Use 5 coins to make 96¢.					

Name_____

Using Combinations of Coins to Pay

Use the coins shown to make each amount.

🖊	HALF DOLLAR	QUARTER	DIME	NICKEL
A. Use 3 coins to make 60¢. What coins did you use?				
B. What other way can you do it?				
C. Use 4 coins to make 40¢. What coins did you use?				
D. What other way can you do it?				
E. Use 4 coins to make 80¢. What coins did you use?				
F. What other way can you do it?				

Name_____

Money Stories

Read each story puzzle.

A. Sean sees a box of magnets on sale for 50 cents. He takes 10 identical coins out of his pocket and buys the magnets.

What coins does he use?

_____

B. Tonia sees a small bag of jacks for 58 cents. She takes 6 coins out of her pocket to pay.

What coins does she use?

_____

C. Dustin sees a toy hammer. He wants to buy it for his little brother. He pulls six coins out of his pocket and pays 54 cents.

What coins does he use?

_____

Money Stories

Read each story puzzle.

A. Matt buys a box of things for doing magic tricks. He takes three coins out of his pocket and pays 80 cents.

What coins could they be?

_____

_____

B. Stacey buys a poster for 52 cents. She uses four coins to buy it.

What coins does she use?

_____

_____

C. **Choose** a price. **Write** a money story about buying the stuffed whale. **Ask** a friend to solve your puzzle.

_____

_____

_____

Name_____

Money Stories

Read each story.

A. Amber put coins into her bank for a
long time. She saved $6.25 in all.
Amber saved $3.55 more than her
sister Holly.

How much did Holly save?

_____

B. Collin and Jason each bought a
watch. Jason paid $4.99 for his
Flip-up Crocodile Watch. That was
$1.20 more than Collin paid for his
Dinosaur Watch.

How much did Collin pay?

_____

C. **Write** a money story about yourself and a friend. **Ask a friend** to solve
your puzzle.

_____

_____

_____

Name_____

Money Stories

Read each story.

A. Darci and Kara fed the horses
    at the fair. Kara's mother gave
    the girls 3 one dollar bills,
    3 quarters, 5 dimes and
    3 nickels. Darci and Kara
    divided the money equally.

   How much money did each girl get?

_____

B. Josh and Ben washed cars one
    Saturday. When they finished,
    they had 3 one dollar bills,
    1 half dollar, three quarters,
    2 dimes and 1 nickel in their
    money box. The boys divided
    the money fairly.

   How much money did each of them get?

_____

C. **Write** a money story about earning money with a friend and dividing it
    equally. **Ask a friend** to solve your puzzle.

_____

_____

_____

Name_____

Money Stories

Read each story puzzle.

A. Eric and Alicia took all the coins out of their pockets. They put the coins together and paid 65 cents for a bag of corn chips. Alicia paid 15 cents more than Eric.

How much did each of them pay?

Eric: _____   Alicia: _____

B. Rachel and Amanda put their money together and bought a package of stickers for $1.60. Rachel paid 20 cents more than Amanda.

How much did each girl pay?

Rachel: _____   Amanda: _____

C. **Write** a money story about buying something with a friend. **Ask a friend** to solve your puzzle.

_____

_____

_____

Coins and Dollar Bills

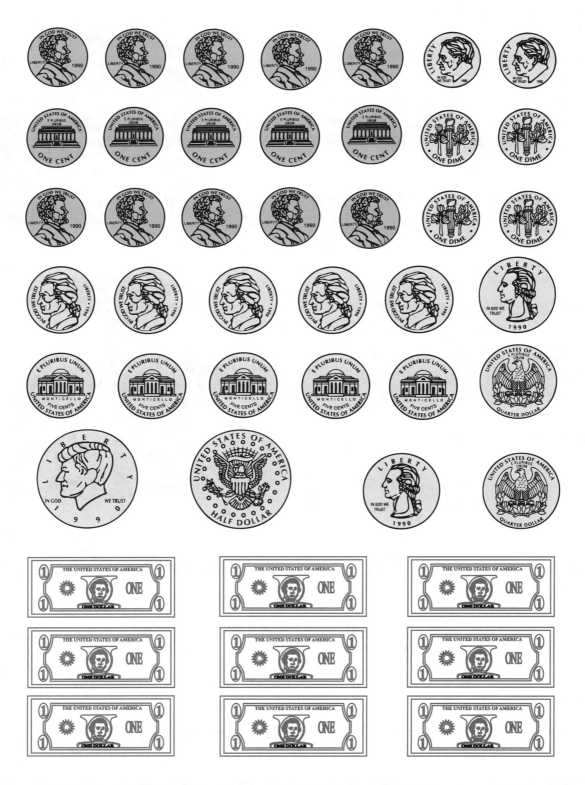

Time Award Certificates

Champion Time Teller!

_____
name

You are a champion time teller because _____

_____

Nice Going!

Signed_____ Date _____

_____
name

Wonderful Work!

You are wonderful because _____

_____

Way to Go!

Signed_____ Date _____

Money Award Certificates

Math Marvel!

_____
name

You are a Math Marvel because _____

_____

Marvelous Job!

Signed_____ Date _____

_____
name

Wonderful Work!

You are a Money Expert because _____

_____

Awesome Work!

Signed_____ Date _____

Answer Key

Page 8

Time to the Hour   Name_____

Face Clocks: Introduction

What is the best way to tell what time it is? **A clock!**

There are all kinds of clocks. **Circle** the ones you have seen.

Answers will vary.

Page 11

Time to the Hour   Name_____

Writing the Time

Learning to tell time is fun! A clock tells us the time.

Write the numbers on the clock face.
Draw the BIG HAND to **12**.
Draw the **little hand** to **5**.

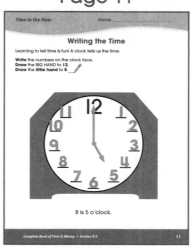

It is 5 o'clock.

Page 12

Time to the Hour   Name_____

Writing the Time

An **hour** is **60 minutes** long.

It takes an **hour** for the BIG HAND to go around the clock.

When the BIG HAND is on **12** and the **little hand** points to a number, that number is **the hour!**

The BIG HAND is on the **12**. **Color** it red.

The **little hand** is on the **8**. **Color** it blue.

The BIG HAND is on ___12___.
The **little hand** is on ___8___.

It is ___8___ o'clock.

Page 13

Time to the Hour   Name_____

Writing the Time

Color each **little hour hand** blue.

Fill in the blanks.

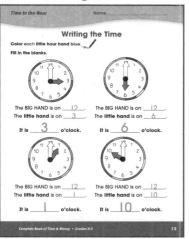

The BIG HAND is on ___12___.   The BIG HAND is on ___12___.
The **little hand** is on ___3___.   The **little hand** is on ___6___.

It is ___3___ o'clock.   It is ___6___ o'clock.

The BIG HAND is on ___12___.   The BIG HAND is on ___12___.
The **little hand** is on ___1___.   The **little hand** is on ___10___.

It is ___1___ o'clock.   It is ___10___ o'clock.

Page 14

Time to the Hour   Name_____

Writing the Time

Color the **little hour hand** blue.

Fill in the blanks.

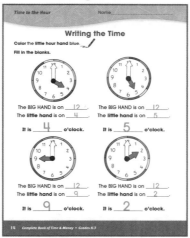

The BIG HAND is on ___12___.   The BIG HAND is on ___12___.
The **little hand** is on ___4___.   The **little hand** is on ___5___.

It is ___4___ o'clock.   It is ___5___ o'clock.

The BIG HAND is on ___12___.   The BIG HAND is on ___12___.
The **little hand** is on ___9___.   The **little hand** is on ___2___.

It is ___9___ o'clock.   It is ___2___ o'clock.

Page 15

Time to the Hour   Name_____

Drawing the Hour Hand

If the BIG HAND is on **12**, it is easy to tell the time.

Look at the **little hand** to see the hour.

Trace the **little hand** to make the hour **10** o'clock.

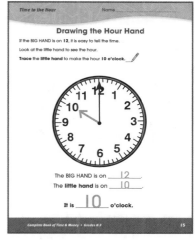

The BIG HAND is on ___12___.
The **little hand** is on ___10___.

It is ___10___ o'clock.

Page 16

Time to the Hour   Name_____

Drawing the Hour Hand

Draw the **little hour hand** on each clock.

8 o'clock   1 o'clock

7 o'clock

Page 17

Time to the Hour   Name_____

Drawing the Hour Hand

Draw the **little hour hand** on each clock.

4 o'clock   11 o'clock

5 o'clock

Page 18

Time to the Hour   Name_____

Drawing the Hour Hand

Draw the **little hour hand** on each clock.

2 o'clock   10 o'clock

9 o'clock

Answer Key

Page 19

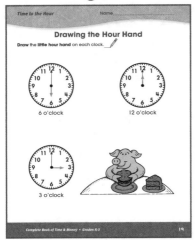

Page 20

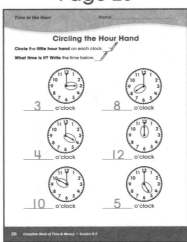

Page 21

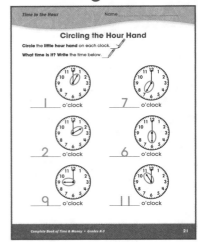

Page 22

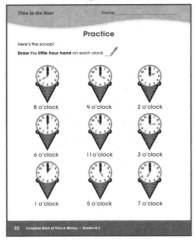

Page 23

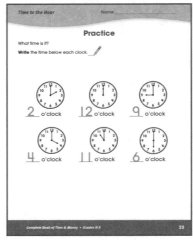

Page 24

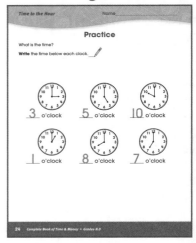

Page 25

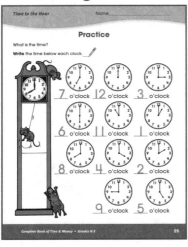

Page 26

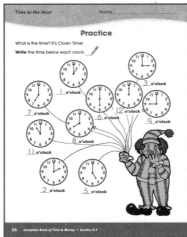

Page 27

Answer Key

Page 28

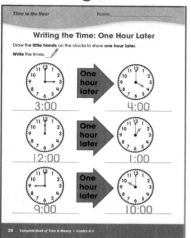

Page 29

Page 30

Page 31

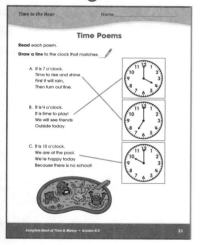

Page 32

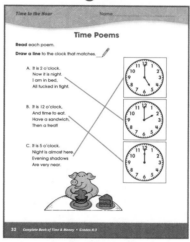

Page 33

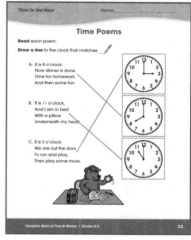

Page 34

Page 35

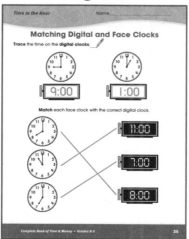

Page 36

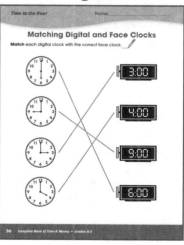

Complete Book of Time & Money • Grades K-3

377

Answer Key

Page 37

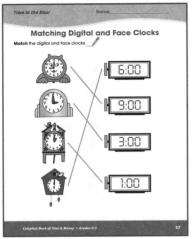

Page 38

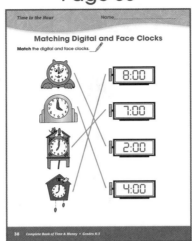

Page 39

Page 40

Page 41

Page 42

Page 43

Page 44

Page 45

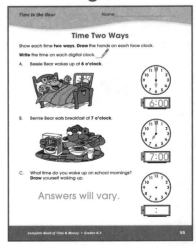

Answer Key

Page 46

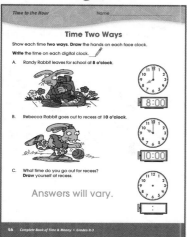

Time to the Hour   Name_____

Time Two Ways

Show each time **two ways**. **Draw** the hands on each face clock.

Write the time on each digital clock.

A. Randy Rabbit leaves for school at **8 o'clock**.

B. Rebecca Rabbit goes out to recess at **10 o'clock**.

C. What time do you go out for recess? **Draw** yourself at recess.

Answers will vary.

Page 47

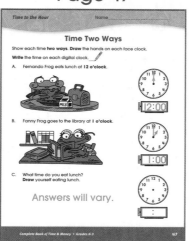

Time to the Hour   Name_____

Time Two Ways

Show each time **two ways**. **Draw** the hands on each face clock.

Write the time on each digital clock.

A. Fernando Frog eats lunch at **12 o'clock**.

B. Fanny Frog goes to the library at **1 o'clock**.

C. What time do you eat lunch? **Draw** yourself eating lunch.

Answers will vary.

Page 48

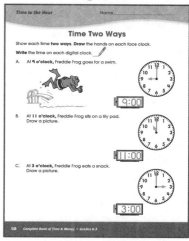

Time to the Hour   Name_____

Time Two Ways

Show each time **two ways**. **Draw** the hands on each face clock.

Write the time on each digital clock.

A. At **9 o'clock**, Freddie Frog goes for a swim.

B. At **11 o'clock**, Freddie Frog sits on a lily pad. Draw a picture.

C. At **3 o'clock**, Freddie Frog eats a snack. Draw a picture.

Page 49

Time to the Hour   Name_____

Time Stories

Read each story. **Draw** the hands on each face clock.

A. At **11:00**, Mouse starts to cook. Yum! Cheese soup is good.

B. At **12 o'clock**, Mouse sets the table. Uh-oh! He drops a spoon.

C. At **7:00**, Mouse reads a book. What a funny story!

D. Time for bed. It is **9 o'clock**, and Mouse is sleepy.

Page 50

Time to the Hour   Name_____

Time Stories

Read each story. **Draw** the hands on each face clock.

A. Rabbit is hungry. It is **6 o'clock**—time for supper and some carrot stew.

B. At **8 o'clock**, Rabbit washes the dishes. Scrub, scrub! The pot is sticky.

C. Rabbit works in his garden. It is **4 o'clock**, and he is picking lettuce.

D. At **5:00**, Rabbit makes a lettuce salad. What a tasty meal!

Page 51

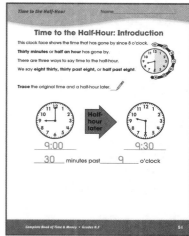

Time to the Half-Hour   Name_____

Time to the Half-Hour: Introduction

This clock face shows the time that has gone by since 8 o'clock.

Thirty minutes or **half an hour** has gone by.

There are three ways to say time to the half-hour.

We say **eight thirty**, **thirty past eight**, or **half past eight**.

Trace the original time and a half-hour later.

9:00   Half-hour later   9:30

30 minutes past 9 o'clock

Page 52

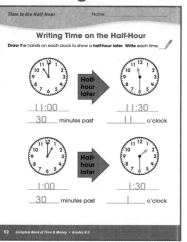

Time to the Half-Hour   Name_____

Writing Time on the Half-Hour

Draw the hands on each clock to show a **half-hour later**. **Write** each time.

11:00   Half-hour later   11:30

30 minutes past 11 o'clock

1:00   Half-hour later   1:30

30 minutes past 1 o'clock

Page 53

Time to the Half-Hour   Name_____

Writing Time on the Half-Hour

What time is it?

half past 2   half past 9

half past 4   half past 12

half past 11   half past 1

Page 54

Time to the Half-Hour   Name_____

Writing Time on the Half-Hour

What time is it?

half past 3   half past 5

half past 7   half past 10

half past 8   half past 6

Answer Key

Page 55

Page 56

Page 57

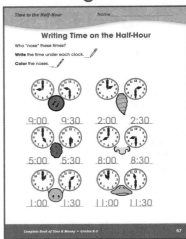

Page 58

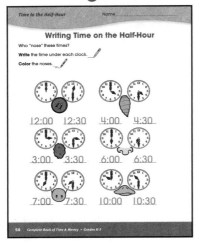

Page 59

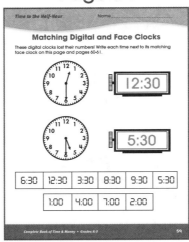

Page 60

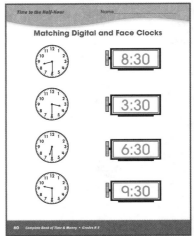

Page 61

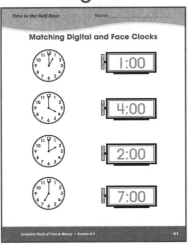

Page 62

Page 63

Answer Key

Page 64

Time to the Half-Hour   Name_____

Drawing the Hour Hand

Say the time. Draw the **little hour hand** on each clock.

3:30   6:30

2:30   9:30

Page 65

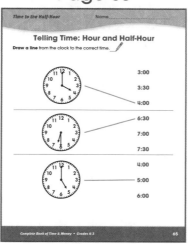

Time to the Half-Hour   Name_____

Telling Time: Hour and Half-Hour

Draw a line from the clock to the correct time.

3:00
3:30
4:00

6:30
7:00
7:30

4:00
5:00
6:00

Page 66

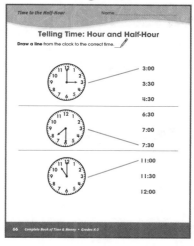

Time to the Half-Hour   Name_____

Telling Time: Hour and Half-Hour

Draw a line from the clock to the correct time.

3:00
3:30
4:30

6:30
7:00
7:30

11:00
11:30
12:00

Page 67

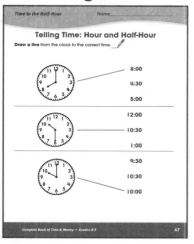

Time to the Half-Hour   Name_____

Telling Time: Hour and Half-Hour

Draw a line from the clock to the correct time.

8:00
4:30
5:00

12:00
10:30
1:00

9:30
10:30
10:00

Page 68

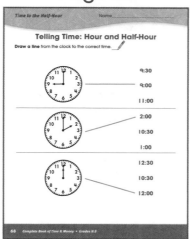

Time to the Half-Hour   Name_____

Telling Time: Hour and Half-Hour

Draw a line from the clock to the correct time.

9:30
9:00
11:00

2:00
10:30
1:00

12:30
10:30
12:00

Page 69

Time to the Half-Hour   Name_____

Writing the Time: Practice

What time is it? It's space time! **Write** the time below each clock.

3:00   9:30   10:30   12:00

8:00   7:30   2:00   4:30

1:30   6:30

7:00   11:00

Page 70

Time to the Half-Hour   Name_____

Writing the Time: Practice

What time is it? It's space time! **Write** the time below each clock.

4:00   9:00   12:30   2:00

7:30   1:00   3:30   5:00

6:00   10:00

11:30   5:30

Page 71

Time to the Half-Hour   Name_____

Writing the Time: Practice

Draw the hands on the sock clocks.

5:30   1:30   7:00

4:30   10:00   3:30

9:30   4:00   2:30

Page 72

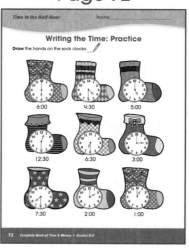

Time to the Half-Hour   Name_____

Writing the Time: Practice

Draw the hands on the sock clocks.

6:00   4:30   5:00

12:30   6:30   3:00

7:30   2:00   1:00

Answer Key

Page 73

Page 74

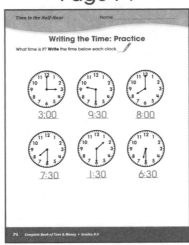

Page 75

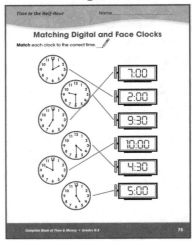

Page 76

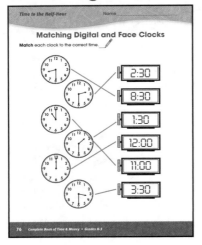

Page 77

Page 78

Page 79

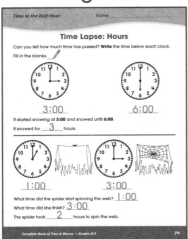

Page 80

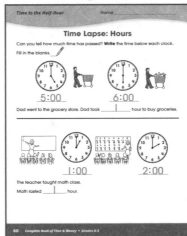

Page 81

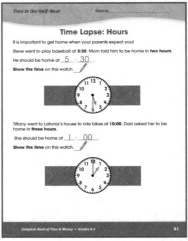

Page 82

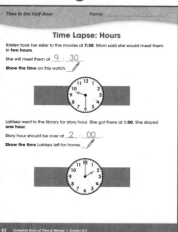

Time to the Half-Hour   Name_____

Time Lapse: Hours

Kristen took her sister to the movies at **7:30**. Mom said she would meet them in **two hours**.

She will meet them at **9** : **30**.

Show the time on this watch.

Latrissa went to the library for story hour. She got there at **1:00**. She stayed **one hour**.

Story hour should be over at **2** : **00**.

Show the time Latrissa left for home.

Page 83

Time to the Half-Hour   Name_____

Drawing the Hour Hand: A Half-Hour Later

Trace and draw the hands on each face clock.

A. At **7:00**, Bill turns the TV on.

What time is it one half-hour later?

B. At **4:00**, we all jump in the car.

What time is it one half-hour later?

Page 84

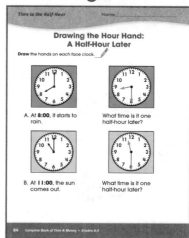

Time to the Half-Hour   Name_____

Drawing the Hour Hand: A Half-Hour Later

Draw the hands on each face clock.

A. At **8:00**, it starts to rain.

What time is it one half-hour later?

B. At **11:00**, the sun comes out.

What time is it one half-hour later?

Page 85

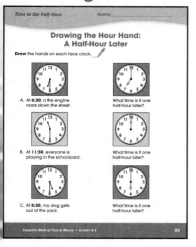

Time to the Half-Hour   Name_____

Drawing the Hour Hand: A Half-Hour Later

Draw the hands on each face clock.

A. At **6:30**, a fire engine roars down the street.

What time is it one half-hour later?

B. At **11:30**, everyone is playing in the schoolyard.

What time is it one half-hour later?

C. At **5:30**, my dog gets out of the yard.

What time is it one half-hour later?

Page 86

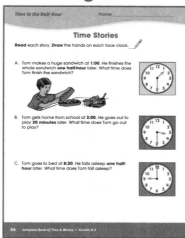

Time to the Half-Hour   Name_____

Time Stories

Read each story. **Draw** the hands on each face clock.

A. Tom makes a huge sandwich at **1:00**. He finishes the whole sandwich **one half-hour** later. What time does Tom finish the sandwich?

B. Tom gets home from school at **3:00**. He goes out to play **30 minutes** later. What time does Tom go out to play?

C. Tom goes to bed at **8:30**. He falls asleep **one half-hour** later. What time does Tom fall asleep?

Page 87

Time to the Half-Hour   Name_____

Time Stories

Read each story. **Draw** the hands on each face clock.

A. Maria walks to the bus stop at **7:00**. She gets on the bus **30 minutes** later. What time does she get on the bus?

B. Maria helps make dinner at **5:30**. Everyone eats **one half-hour** later. What time does everyone eat?

C. Maria's family plays a game at **6:00**. They stop playing **30 minutes** later. What time do they stop playing?

Page 88

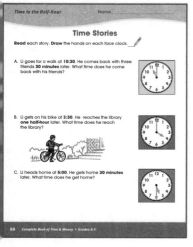

Time to the Half-Hour   Name_____

Time Stories

Read each story. **Draw** the hands on each face clock.

A. Li goes for a walk at **10:30**. He comes back with three friends **30 minutes** later. What time does he come back with his friends?

B. Li gets on his bike at **3:30**. He reaches the library **one half-hour** later. What time does he reach the library?

C. Li heads home at **5:00**. He gets home **30 minutes** later. What time does he get home?

Page 89

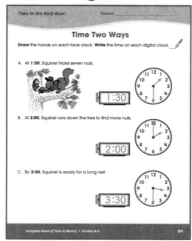

Time to the Half-Hour   Name_____

Time Two Ways

Draw the hands on each face clock. **Write** the time on each digital clock.

A. At **1:30**, Squirrel hides seven nuts.

1:30

B. At **2:00**, Squirrel runs down the tree to find more nuts.

2:00

C. By **3:30**, Squirrel is ready for a long rest.

3:30

Page 90

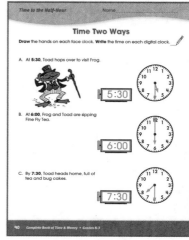

Time to the Half-Hour   Name_____

Time Two Ways

Draw the hands on each face clock. **Write** the time on each digital clock.

A. At **5:30**, Toad hops over to visit Frog.

5:30

B. At **6:00**, Frog and Toad are sipping Fine Fly Tea.

6:00

C. By **7:30**, Toad heads home, full of tea and bug cakes.

7:30

Answer Key

Page 91

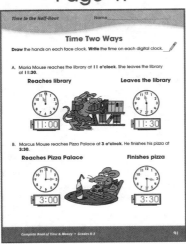

Time to the Half-Hour   Name_____

Time Two Ways

Draw the hands on each face clock. **Write** the time on each digital clock.

A. Maria Mouse reaches the library at **11 o'clock**. She leaves the library at **11:30**.

Reaches library   **Leaves the library**

`11:00`   `11:30`

B. Marcus Mouse reaches Pizza Palace at **3 o'clock**. He finishes his pizza at **3:30**.

Reaches Pizza Palace   **Finishes pizza**

`3:00`   `3:30`

Page 92

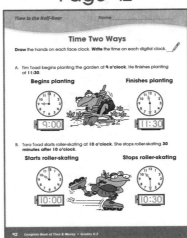

Time to the Half-Hour   Name_____

Time Two Ways

Draw the hands on each face clock. **Write** the time on each digital clock.

A. Tim Toad begins planting the garden at **9 o'clock**. He finishes planting at **11:30**.

Begins planting   **Finishes planting**

`9:00`   `11:30`

B. Tara Toad starts roller-skating at **10 o'clock**. She stops roller-skating **30 minutes after 10 o'clock**.

Starts roller-skating   **Stops roller-skating**

`10:00`   `10:30`

Page 93

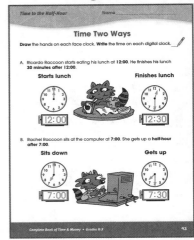

Time to the Half-Hour   Name_____

Time Two Ways

Draw the hands on each face clock. **Write** the time on each digital clock.

A. Ricardo Raccoon starts eating his lunch at **12:00**. He finishes his lunch **30 minutes after 12:00**.

Starts lunch   **Finishes lunch**

`12:00`   `12:30`

B. Rachel Raccoon sits at the computer at **7:00**. She gets up a **half-hour after 7:00**.

Sits down   **Gets up**

`7:00`   `7:30`

Page 94

Time to the Half-Hour   Name_____

Time Stories

Read the story. **Write** the time two ways.

Bear is going on a picnic today with his brother and sister. They leave for the park at **9:00**. They get to the park at **10:00**. Bear helps carry the food to a picnic table. Then, he gets out his kite. Bear flies his kite at **10:30**. Later, at **11:30**, everyone has a picnic lunch!

Put the story in order by writing what time Bear does each thing.

Leaves for the park   **Gets to the park**

`9:00`   `10:00`

Flies kite   **Eats lunch**

`10:30`   `11:30`

Page 95

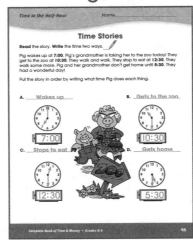

Time to the Half-Hour   Name_____

Time Stories

Read the story. **Write** the time two ways.

Pig wakes up at **7:00**. Pig's grandmother is taking her to the zoo today! They get to the zoo at **10:30**. They walk and walk. They stop to eat at **12:30**. They walk some more. Pig and her grandmother don't get home until **5:30**. They had a wonderful day!

Put the story in order by writing what time Pig does each thing.

A. _Wakes up_   B. _Gets to the zoo_

`7:00`   `10:30`

C. _Stops to eat_   D. _Gets home_

`12:30`   `5:30`

Page 96

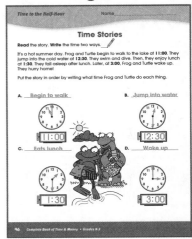

Time to the Half-Hour   Name_____

Time Stories

Read the story. **Write** the time two ways.

It's a hot summer day. Frog and Turtle begin to walk to the lake at **11:00**. They jump into the cold water at **12:30**. They swim and dive. Then, they enjoy lunch at **1:30**. They fall asleep after lunch. Later, at **3:00**, Frog and Turtle wake up. They hurry home!

Put the story in order by writing what time Frog and Turtle do each thing.

A. _Begin to walk_   B. _Jump into water_

`11:00`   `12:30`

C. _Eats lunch_   D. _Wake up_

`1:30`   `3:00`

Page 97

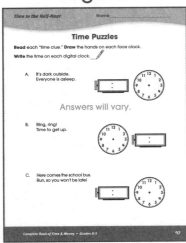

Time to the Half-Hour   Name_____

Time Puzzles

Read each "time clue." **Draw** the hands on each face clock.

Write the time on each digital clock.

A. It's dark outside. Everyone is asleep.

Answers will vary.

B. Ring, ring! Time to get up.

C. Here comes the school bus. Run, so you won't be late!

Page 98

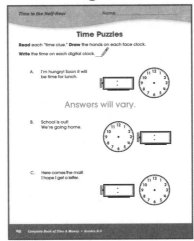

Time to the Half-Hour   Name_____

Time Puzzles

Read each "time clue." **Draw** the hands on each face clock.

Write the time on each digital clock.

A. I'm hungry! Soon it will be time for lunch.

Answers will vary.

B. School is out! We're going home.

C. Here comes the mail! I hope I get a letter.

Page 99

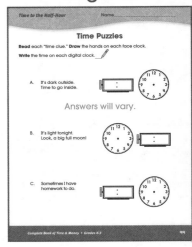

Time to the Half-Hour   Name_____

Time Puzzles

Read each "time clue." **Draw** the hands on each face clock.

Write the time on each digital clock.

A. It's dark outside. Time to go inside.

Answers will vary.

B. It's light tonight. Look, a big full moon!

C. Sometimes I have homework to do.

Page 100

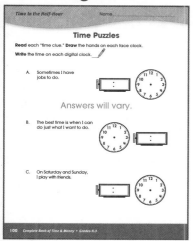

Time Puzzles

Read each "time clue." Draw the hands on each face clock.
Write the time on each digital clock.

A. Sometimes I have jobs to do.

Answers will vary.

B. The best time is when I can do just what I want to do.

C. On Saturday and Sunday, I play with friends.

Page 101

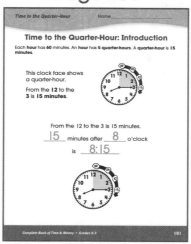

Time to the Quarter-Hour: Introduction

Each hour has 60 minutes. An hour has 4 quarter-hours. A quarter-hour is 15 minutes.

This clock face shows a quarter-hour.
From the 12 to the 3 is 15 minutes.

From the 12 to the 3 is 15 minutes.

__15__ minutes after __8__ o'clock
is __8:15__

Page 102

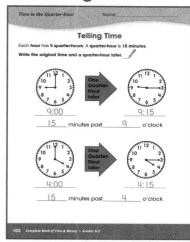

Telling Time

Each hour has 4 quarter-hours. A quarter-hour is 15 minutes.
Write the original time and a quarter-hour later.

9:00 → One Quarter-Hour later → 9:15
__15__ minutes past __9__ o'clock

4:00 → One Quarter-Hour later → 4:15
__15__ minutes past __4__ o'clock

Page 103

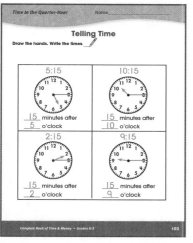

Telling Time

Draw the hands. Write the times.

5:15
__15__ minutes after __5__ o'clock

10:15
__15__ minutes after __10__ o'clock

2:15
__15__ minutes after __2__ o'clock

9:15
__15__ minutes after __9__ o'clock

Page 104

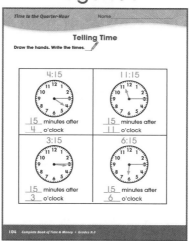

Telling Time

Draw the hands. Write the times.

4:15
__15__ minutes after __4__ o'clock

11:15
__15__ minutes after __11__ o'clock

3:15
__15__ minutes after __3__ o'clock

6:15
__15__ minutes after __6__ o'clock

Page 105

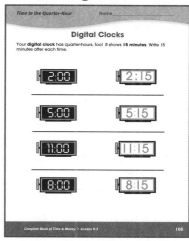

Digital Clocks

Your digital clock has quarter-hours, too! It shows 15 minutes. Write 15 minutes after each time.

2:00   2:15
5:00   5:15
11:00   11:15
8:00   8:15

Page 106

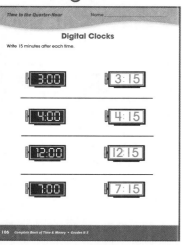

Digital Clocks

Write 15 minutes after each time.

3:00   3:15
4:00   4:15
12:00   12:15
7:00   7:15

Page 107

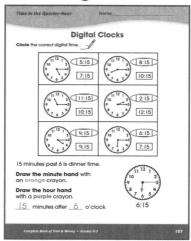

Digital Clocks

Circle the correct digital time.

5:15 / 7:15
8:15 / 10:15
11:15 / 10:15
2:15 / 12:15
4:15 / 9:15
6:15 / 7:15

15 minutes past 6 is dinner time.
Draw the minute hand with an orange crayon.
Draw the hour hand with a purple crayon.
__15__ minutes after __6__ o'clock
6:15

Page 108

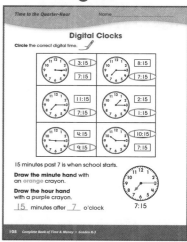

Digital Clocks

Circle the correct digital time.

3:15 / 7:15
8:15 / 7:15
11:15 / 7:15
2:15 / 1:15
4:15 / 9:15
10:15 / 7:15

15 minutes past 7 is when school starts.
Draw the minute hand with an orange crayon.
Draw the hour hand with a purple crayon.
__15__ minutes after __7__ o'clock
7:15

Answer Key

Page 109

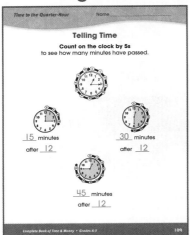

Page 110

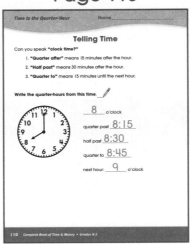

Page 111

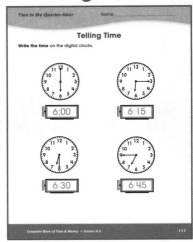

Page 112

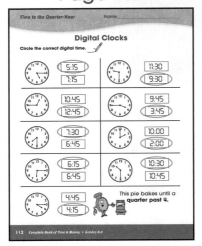

Page 113

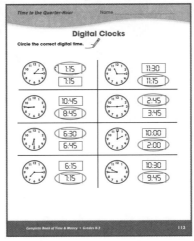

Page 114

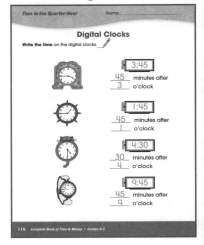

Page 115

Page 116

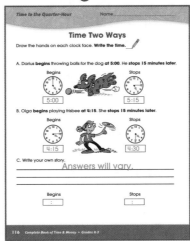

Page 117

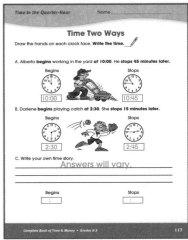

Answer Key

Page 118

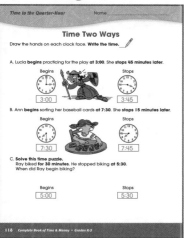

Page 119

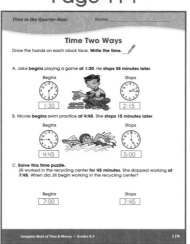

Page 120

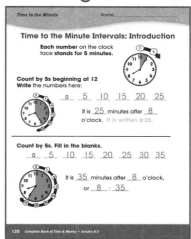

Page 121

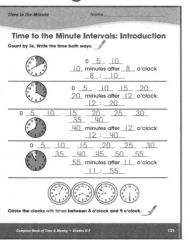

Page 122

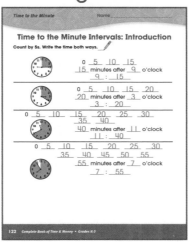

Page 123

Page 124

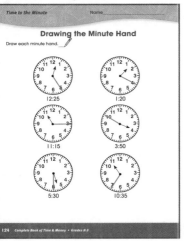

Page 125

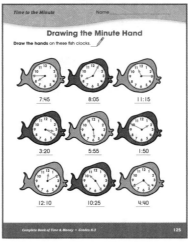

Page 126

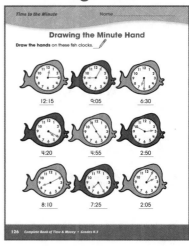

Page 127

Page 128

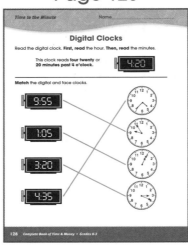

Page 129

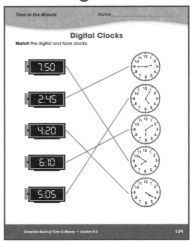

Page 130

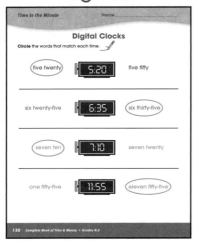

Page 131

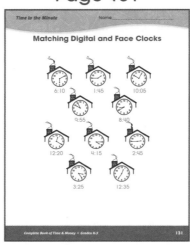

Page 133

Page 135

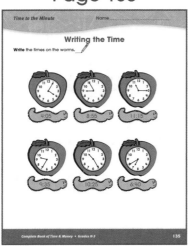

Page 136

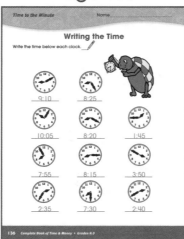

Page 137

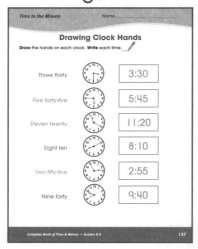

Page 138

Time to the Minute   Name _____

Drawing Clock Hands

Draw the hands on each clock. **Write** each time.

One oh-five	1:05
Three fifteen	3:15
Six fifty-five	6:55
Seven fifty	7:50
Four twenty-five	4:25
Five thirty	5:30

138   Complete Book of Time & Money • Grades K-3

Page 139

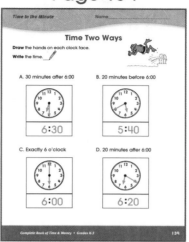

Time to the Minute   Name _____

Time Two Ways

Draw the hands on each clock face.
Write the time.

A. 30 minutes after 6:00   **6:30**
B. 20 minutes before 6:00   **5:40**
C. Exactly 6 o'clock   **6:00**
D. 20 minutes after 6:00   **6:20**

Complete Book of Time & Money • Grades K-3   139

Page 140

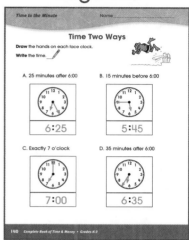

Time to the Minute   Name _____

Time Two Ways

Draw the hands on each face clock.
Write the time.

A. 25 minutes after 6:00   **6:25**
B. 15 minutes before 6:00   **5:45**
C. Exactly 7 o'clock   **7:00**
D. 35 minutes after 6:00   **6:35**

140   Complete Book of Time & Money • Grades K-3

Page 141

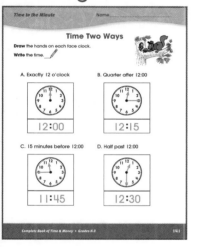

Time to the Minute   Name _____

Time Two Ways

Draw the hands on each face clock.
Write the time.

A. Exactly 12 o'clock   **12:00**
B. Quarter after 12:00   **12:15**
C. 15 minutes before 12:00   **11:45**
D. Half past 12:00   **12:30**

Complete Book of Time & Money • Grades K-3   141

Page 142

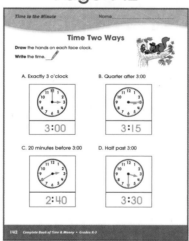

Time to the Minute   Name _____

Time Two Ways

Draw the hands on each face clock.
Write the time.

A. Exactly 3 o'clock   **3:00**
B. Quarter after 3:00   **3:15**
C. 20 minutes before 3:00   **2:40**
D. Half past 3:00   **3:30**

142   Complete Book of Time & Money • Grades K-3

Page 143

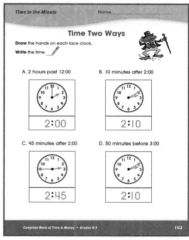

Time to the Minute   Name _____

Time Two Ways

Draw the hands on each face clock.
Write the time.

A. 2 hours past 12:00   **2:00**
B. 10 minutes after 2:00   **2:10**
C. 45 minutes after 2:00   **2:45**
D. 50 minutes before 3:00   **2:10**

Complete Book of Time & Money • Grades K-3   143

Page 144

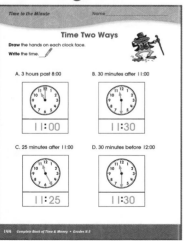

Time to the Minute   Name _____

Time Two Ways

Draw the hands on each clock face.
Write the time.

A. 3 hours past 8:00   **11:00**
B. 30 minutes after 11:00   **11:30**
C. 25 minutes after 11:00   **11:25**
D. 30 minutes before 12:00   **11:30**

144   Complete Book of Time & Money • Grades K-3

Page 145

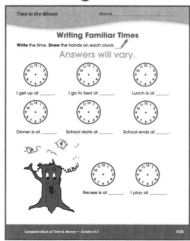

Time to the Minute   Name _____

Writing Familiar Times

Write the time. **Draw** the hands on each clock.

Answers will vary.

I get up at _____.   I go to bed at _____.   Lunch is at _____.

Dinner is at _____.   School starts at _____.   School ends at _____.

Recess is at _____.   I play at _____.

Complete Book of Time & Money • Grades K-3   145

Page 146

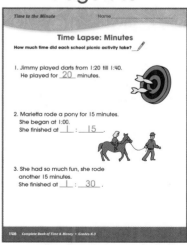

Time to the Minute   Name _____

Time Lapse: Minutes

How much time did each school picnic activity take?

1. Jimmy played darts from 1:20 till 1:40.
   He played for __20__ minutes.

2. Marietta rode a pony for 15 minutes.
   She began at 1:00.
   She finished at _1_ : _15_.

3. She had so much fun, she rode
   another 15 minutes.
   She finished at _1_ : _30_.

146   Complete Book of Time & Money • Grades K-3

Page 147

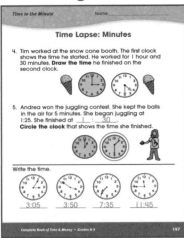

Time Lapse: Minutes

4. Tim worked at the snow cone booth. The first clock shows the time he started. He worked for 1 hour and 30 minutes. **Draw the time** he finished on the second clock.

5. Andrea won the juggling contest. She kept the balls in the air for 5 minutes. She began juggling at 1:25. She finished at __1__ : __30__. **Circle the clock** that shows the time she finished.

Write the time.

3:05   3:50   7:35   11:45

Page 148

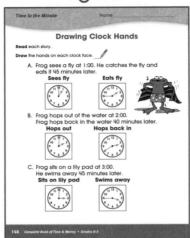

Drawing Clock Hands

Read each story.
Draw the hands on each clock face.

A. Frog sees a fly at 1:00. He catches the fly and eats it 45 minutes later.
Sees fly   **Eats fly**

B. Frog hops out of the water at 2:00. Frog hops back in the water 40 minutes later.
Hops out   **Hops back in**

C. Frog sits on a lily pad at 3:00. He swims away 45 minutes later.
Sits on lily pad   **Swims away**

Page 149

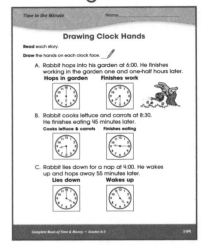

Drawing Clock Hands

Read each story.
Draw the hands on each clock face.

A. Rabbit hops into his garden at 6:00. He finishes working in the garden one and one-half hours later.
Hops in garden   **Finishes work**

B. Rabbit cooks lettuce and carrots at 8:30. He finishes eating 45 minutes later.
Cooks lettuce & carrots   **Finishes eating**

C. Rabbit lies down for a nap at 4:00. He wakes up and hops away 55 minutes later.
Lies down   **Wakes up**

Page 150

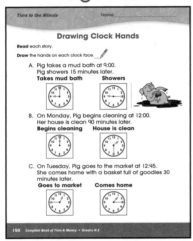

Drawing Clock Hands

Read each story.
Draw the hands on each clock face.

A. Pig takes a mud bath at 9:00. Pig showers 15 minutes later.
Takes mud bath   **Showers**

B. On Monday, Pig begins cleaning at 12:00. Her house is clean 90 minutes later.
Begins cleaning   **House is clean**

C. On Tuesday, Pig goes to the market at 12:45. She comes home with a basket full of goodies 30 minutes later.
Goes to market   **Comes home**

Page 151

Time Stories

Read the story. **Write** each time.

Val and Phil go out to the backyard at 6:00. They put up their tent. This takes them 1 hour and 30 minutes. They get in the tent and talk for 1 hour. Then they fall asleep. They sleep for 2 hours, until a dog barks and wakes them up.

A. Go to backyard   6:00
B. Finish putting up tent   7:30
C. Fall asleep   8:30
D. Dog barks   10:30
E. How long are Val and Phil in the yard before the dog wakes them up?
__4__ hours __30__ minutes

Page 152

Time Stories

Read the story. **Write** each time.

Mike and Maria leave home at 3:30. They ride their bikes to the ice-skating rink. This takes one half-hour. They skate and leave the rink 2 hours later. They get on their bikes and arrive home 40 minutes after leaving the rink.

A. Leave home   3:30
B. Arrive at rink   4:00
C. Leave rink   6:00
D. Arrive home   6:40
E. How long does Mike and Maria's trip to the skating rink and back take?
__3__ hours __10__ minutes

Page 153

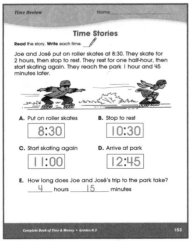

Time Stories

Read the story. **Write** each time.

Joe and José put on roller skates at 8:30. They skate for 2 hours, then stop to rest. They rest for one half-hour, then start skating again. They reach the park 1 hour and 45 minutes later.

A. Put on roller skates   8:30
B. Stop to rest   10:30
C. Start skating again   11:00
D. Arrive at park   12:45
E. How long does Joe and José's trip to the park take?
__4__ hours __15__ minutes

Page 154

Time Stories

Read the story. **Write** each time.

Andrea took her dog for a walk. They left home at 5:30. They walked for 20 minutes. What time did they get home?

A. Leave home   5:30
B. Get home   5:50

Rhiannon and her mother made cookies. They put the cookies in the oven at 7:15. After 10 minutes they took the cookies out of the oven. Yum! What time did they take them out?

C. Cookies in oven   7:15
D. Cookies out of oven   7:25

Anita played table tennis with her brother for 30 minutes. They stopped playing at 4:30. When did Anita begin playing table tennis?

E. Begin playing   4:00
F. Stop playing   4:30

Page 155

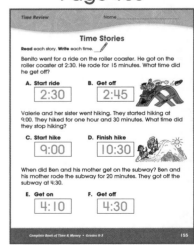

Time Stories

Read each story. **Write** each time.

Benito went for a ride on the roller coaster. He got on the roller coaster at 2:30. He rode for 15 minutes. What time did he get off?

A. Start ride   2:30
B. Get off   2:45

Valerie and her sister went hiking. They started hiking at 9:00. They hiked for one hour and 30 minutes. What time did they stop hiking?

C. Start hike   9:00
D. Finish hike   10:30

When did Ben and his mother get on the subway? Ben and his mother rode the subway for 20 minutes. They got off the subway at 4:30.

E. Get on   4:10
F. Get off   4:30

Page 156

Time Stories

Read the story. **Write** each time.

Andrea and her sister walked by the lake. They started walking at 2:15. They walked for one hour and 15 minutes. What time did they stop walking?

A. Start walking `2:15`　**B. Stop walking** `3:30`

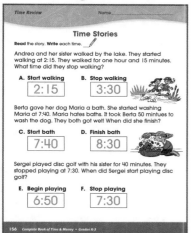

Berta gave her dog Maria a bath. She started washing Maria at 7:40. Maria hates baths. It took Berta 50 minutes to wash the dog. They both got wet! When did she finish?

C. Start bath `7:40`　**D. Finish bath** `8:30`

Sergei played disc golf with his sister for 40 minutes. They stopped playing at 7:30. When did Sergei start playing disc golf?

E. Begin playing `6:50`　**F. Stop playing** `7:30`

156　Complete Book of Time & Money • Grades K-3

Page 157

Time Stories

Read the story. **Write** each time.

Erin and her brother Harry were shopping for dinner. First they went into the bakery at 5:00 to buy fresh bread. This took 5 minutes. Next they walked to the market for vegetables and cereal. This took them 20 minutes. Then they walked next door for a treat at Fanny's Famous Fudge. This took them 15 minutes. Then they met their brother Andrew outside.

A. Go into bakery `5:00`　**B. Leave bakery** `5:05`

C. Leave market `5:25`　**D. Meet Andrew** `5:40`

E. How long had Erin and Harry been shopping before they saw Andrew?
40 minutes

F. Write your own story about shopping on another sheet of paper. What do you do, and how long does each thing take? Make up a starting time. Use a clock to find the ending time.

Complete Book of Time & Money • Grades K-3　157

Page 158

Time Stories

Read the story. **Write** each time.

Hanna and Shawn got to the fair at 3:00. They threw balls at the clown's pocket for 10 minutes. No luck! Then they rode the Big Dipper for 30 minutes. They got wet! After this they ate pizza for 15 minutes. Then they saw their friend Mary.

A. Arrive at the fair `3:00`　**B. Stop throwing balls** `3:10`

C. Stop riding Big Dipper `3:40`　**D. See Mary** `3:55`

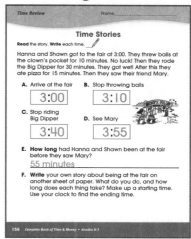

E. How long had Hanna and Shawn been at the fair before they saw Mary?
55 minutes

F. Write your own story about being at the fair on another sheet of paper. What do you do, and how long does each thing take? Make up a starting time. Use your clock to find the ending time.

158　Complete Book of Time & Money • Grades K-3

Page 159

Time Stories

Read the story. **Write** each time.

Valerie and Angela got off the bus at the mall. It was 12:30. First they went to Toby's Toys & Games. They looked at toys for 20 minutes. Then they spent 40 minutes walking to Yummy Yogurt and having a snack. Then they looked at shoes in The Shoe Factory for 15 minutes. They met Angela's sister outside the Shoe Factory.

A. Arrive at mall `12:30`　**B. Leave toy store** `12:50`

C. Leave Yummy Yogurt `1:30`　**D. See Angela's sister** `1:45`

E. How long had Valerie and Angela been at the mall when they saw Angela's sister?
1 hour and 15 minutes

F. Write your own story about shopping on another sheet of paper. What do you do, and how long does each thing take? Make up a starting time. Use your clock to find the ending time.

Complete Book of Time & Money • Grades K-3　159

Page 160

Time Puzzles

Write times that fit each time clue.

A. Between 11:00 and 12:00
`[  :  ]`

Answers will vary.

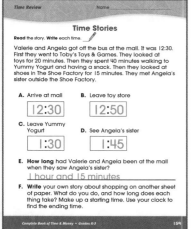

7:15 is my bedtime.

B. Between 30 minutes after 2:00 and 3:00
`[  :  ]`

C. After a quarter-past 7:00 and before 8:00
`[  :  ]`

D. **Write** your own time clues. **Ask a friend** to solve your time puzzle!
Answers will vary.

160　Complete Book of Time & Money • Grades K-3

Page 161

Time Puzzles

Write times that fit each time clue.

A. Between 4:15 and 5:15
`[  :  ]`

Answers will vary.

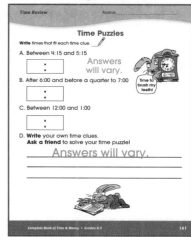

Time to brush my teeth!

B. After 6:00 and before a quarter to 7:00
`[  :  ]`

C. Between 12:00 and 1:00
`[  :  ]`

D. **Write** your own time clues. **Ask a friend** to solve your time puzzle!
Answers will vary.

Complete Book of Time & Money • Grades K-3　161

Page 162

Time Puzzles

Write times that fit each time clue.

A. After 3:00 and before 3:40
`[  :  ]`

Answers will vary.

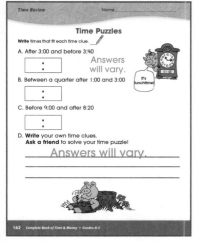

It's lunchtime!

B. Between a quarter after 1:00 and 3:00
`[  :  ]`

C. Before 9:00 and after 8:20
`[  :  ]`

D. **Write** your own time clues. **Ask a friend** to solve your time puzzle!
Answers will vary.

162　Complete Book of Time & Money • Grades K-3

Page 163

Telling Time: Using Charts

BIG TEN MOVIES

Mark's Great Adventure	12:15	3:00	5:30
The Mad Hatter Returns	12:45	3:30	5:45
Morris and the Magic Van	1:30	4:15	6:45

Use the chart. Find the movie that each pair saw.

Write the time that the movie started.

A. Barry and his brother went to the movie that began closest to 4:00.
Movie: Morris and the Magic Van
Began at: 4:15

B. Andrea and her friend went to the movie that began closest to 1:00.
Movie: The Mad Hatter Returns
Began at: 12:45

C. Ismelda and her mom went to the movie that began closest to 6:00.
Movie: The Mad Hatter Returns
Began at: 5:45

D. **Write** your own time puzzle about Big Ten Movies on another sheet of paper. Ask a friend to solve your time puzzle.

Complete Book of Time & Money • Grades K-3　163

Page 164

Telling Time: Using Charts

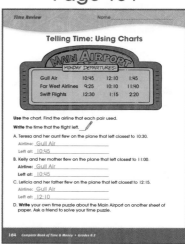

MAIN AIRPORT
MONDAY DEPARTURES

Gull Air	10:45	12:10	1:45
Far West Airlines	9:25	10:10	11:40
Swift Flights	12:30	1:15	2:20

Use the chart. Find the airline that each pair used.

Write the time that the flight left.

A. Teresa and her aunt flew on the plane that left closest to 10:30.
Airline: Gull Air
Left at: 10:45

B. Kelly and her mother flew on the plane that left closest to 11:00.
Airline: Gull Air
Left at: 10:45

C. Leticia and her father flew on the plane that left closest to 12:15.
Airline: Gull Air
Left at: 12:10

D. **Write** your own time puzzle about the Main Airport on another sheet of paper. Ask a friend to solve your time puzzle.

164　Complete Book of Time & Money • Grades K-3

Page 165

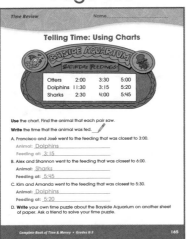

Page 167

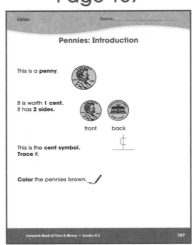

Page 168

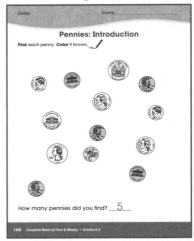

Page 169

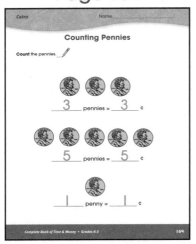

Page 170

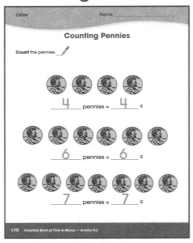

Page 171

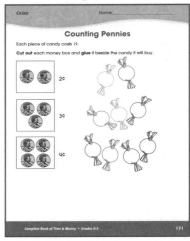

Page 173

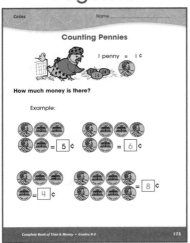

Page 174

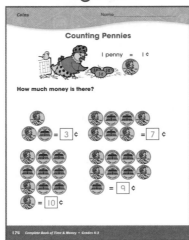

Page 175

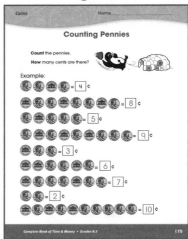

Answer Key

Page 176

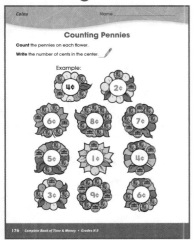

Page 177

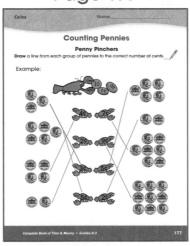

Page 178

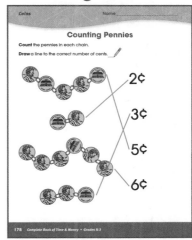

Page 179

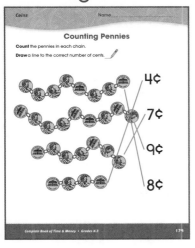

Page 180

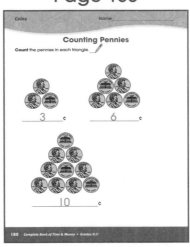

Page 181

Page 182

Page 183

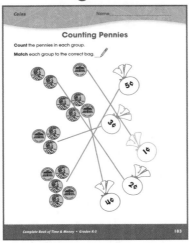

Page 184

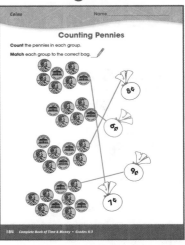

Answer Key

Page 185

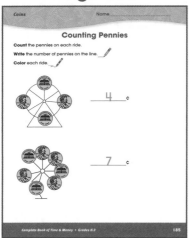

Page 186

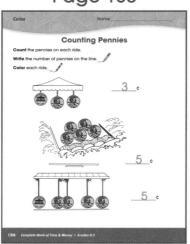

Page 187

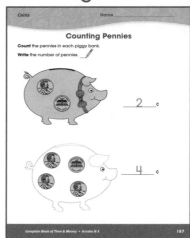

Page 188

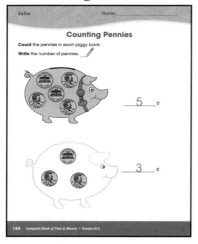

Page 189

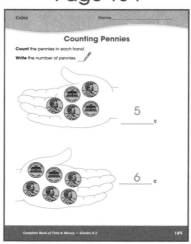

Page 190

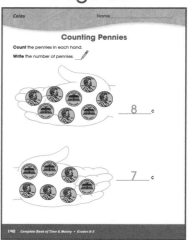

Page 191

Page 192

Page 193

Answer Key

Page 194

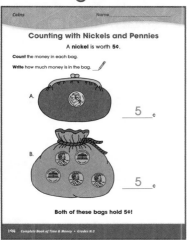

Page 195

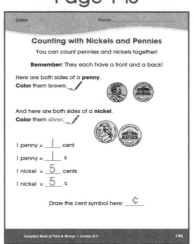

Page 196

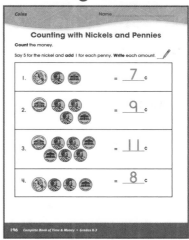

Page 197

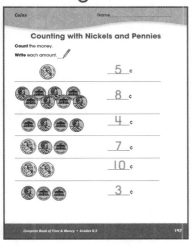

Page 198

Page 199

Page 200

Page 201

Page 202

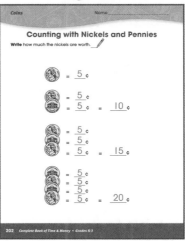

Answer Key

Page 203

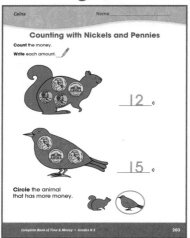

Coins   Name_____

Counting with Nickels and Pennies

Count the money.

Write each amount.

12 ¢

15 ¢

Circle the animal that has more money.

Page 204

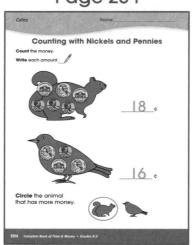

Coins   Name_____

Counting with Nickels and Pennies

Count the money.

Write each amount.

18 ¢

16 ¢

Circle the animal that has more money.

Page 205

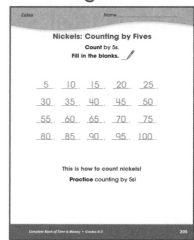

Coins   Name_____

Nickels: Counting by Fives

Count by 5s.

Fill in the blanks.

5, 10, 15, 20, 25,
30, 35, 40, 45, 50,
55, 60, 65, 70, 75,
80, 85, 90, 95, 100.

This is how to count nickels!

Practice counting by 5s!

Page 206

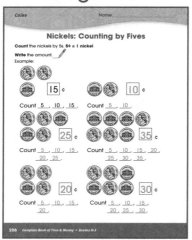

Coins   Name_____

Nickels: Counting by Fives

Count the nickels by 5s. 5¢ = 1 nickel

Write the amount.

Example:

15 ¢   10 ¢

Count 5, 10, 15.   Count 5, 10.

25 ¢   35 ¢

Count 5, 10, 15.   Count 5, 10, 15,
20, 25.   25, 30, 35.

20 ¢   30 ¢

Count 5, 10, 15,   Count 5, 10, 15,
20.   20, 25, 30.

Page 207

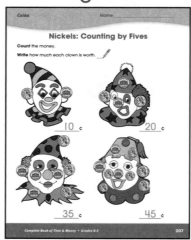

Coins   Name_____

Nickels: Counting by Fives

Count the money.

Write how much each clown is worth.

10 ¢   20 ¢

35 ¢   45 ¢

Page 208

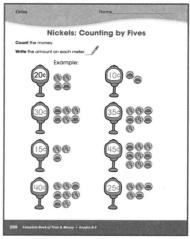

Coins   Name_____

Nickels: Counting by Fives

Count the money.

Write the amount on each meter.

Example:

20¢   10¢

30¢   35¢

15¢   45¢

40¢   25¢

Page 209

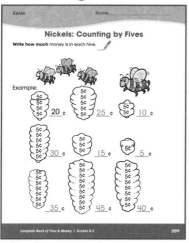

Coins   Name_____

Nickels: Counting by Fives

Write how much money is in each hive.

Example:

20 ¢   25 ¢   10 ¢

30 ¢   15 ¢   5 ¢

35 ¢   45 ¢   40 ¢

Page 210

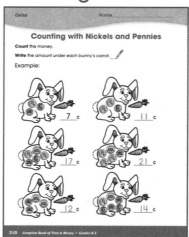

Coins   Name_____

Counting with Nickels and Pennies

Count the money.

Write the amount under each bunny's carrot.

Example:

7 ¢   11 ¢

17 ¢   21 ¢

12 ¢   14 ¢

Page 211

Coins   Name_____

Counting with Nickels and Pennies

Count the money.

Write the amount under each bunny's carrot.

Example:

6 ¢   25 ¢

13 ¢   22 ¢

13 ¢   12 ¢

Page 212

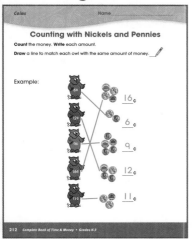

Page 213

Page 214

Page 215

Page 216

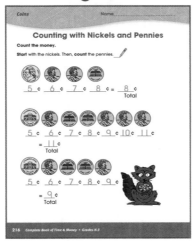

Page 217

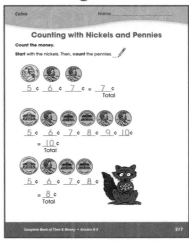

Page 218

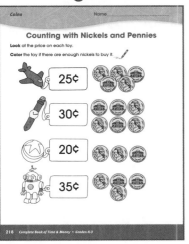

Page 219

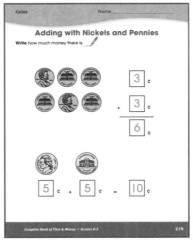

Page 220

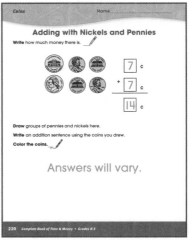

Page 221

Page 222

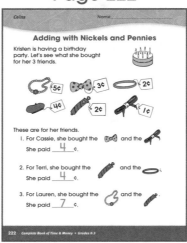

Page 223

Page 224

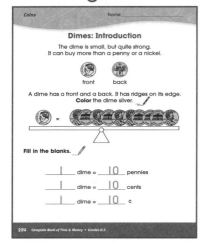

Page 225

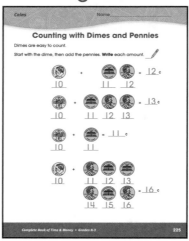

Page 226

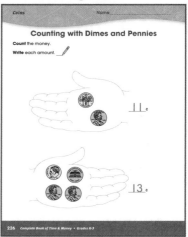

Page 227

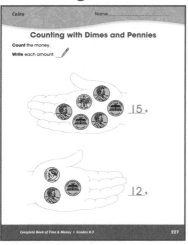

Page 228

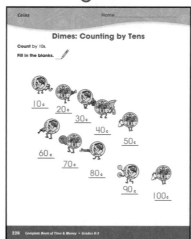

Page 229

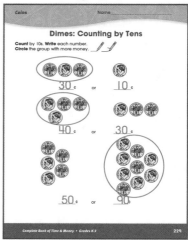

Answer Key

Page 230

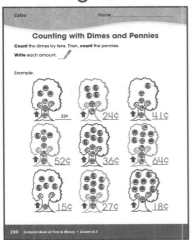

Coins — Counting with Dimes and Pennies

Count the dimes by tens. Then, count the pennies.

Write each amount.

Example: 33¢ 24¢ 41¢

52¢ 36¢ 64¢

15¢ 27¢ 18¢

Page 231

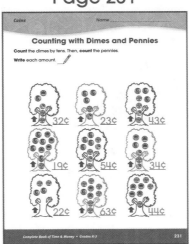

Coins — Counting with Dimes and Pennies

Count the dimes by tens. Then, count the pennies.

Write each amount.

32¢ 23¢ 43¢

19¢ 54¢ 34¢

22¢ 63¢ 44¢

Page 232

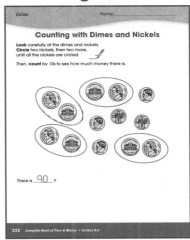

Coins — Counting with Dimes and Nickels

Look carefully at the dimes and nickels. Circle two nickels, then two more, until all the nickels are circled.

Then, count by 10s to see how much money there is.

There is 90 ¢

Page 233

Coins — Counting with Dimes and Nickels

Count the money.

Write each amount.

10 ¢ 20 ¢ 25 ¢ 30 ¢ 35 ¢ 35 ¢ Total

10 ¢ 20 ¢ 30 ¢ 40 ¢ 50 ¢ 55 ¢

60 ¢ 65 ¢ 70 ¢ 70 ¢ Total

What coins does Raccoon have?

I'm counting my money. 10¢, 20¢, 30¢, 35¢, 40¢, 45¢, 50¢...

10¢ 10¢ 10¢
5¢ 5¢ 5¢ 5¢

Page 234

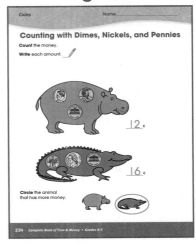

Coins — Counting with Dimes, Nickels, and Pennies

Count the money.

Write each amount.

12 ¢

16 ¢

Circle the animal that has more money.

Page 235

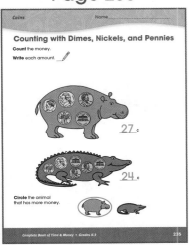

Coins — Counting with Dimes, Nickels, and Pennies

Count the money.

Write each amount.

27 ¢

24 ¢

Circle the animal that has more money.

Page 236

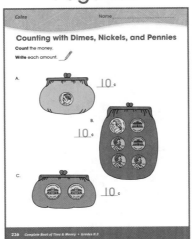

Coins — Counting with Dimes, Nickels, and Pennies

Count the money.

Write each amount.

A. 10 ¢

B. 10 ¢

C. 10 ¢

Page 237

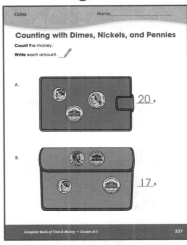

Coins — Counting with Dimes, Nickels, and Pennies

Count the money.

Write each amount.

A. 20 ¢

B. 17 ¢

Answer Key

Page 238

Coins   Name

Counting with Dimes, Nickels, and Pennies

Count the money.

Write each amount.

16¢

18¢

238   Complete Book of Time & Money • Grades K-3

Page 239

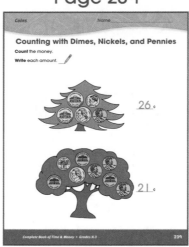

Coins   Name

Counting with Dimes, Nickels, and Pennies

Count the money.

Write each amount.

26¢

21¢

Complete Book of Time & Money • Grades K-3   239

Page 240

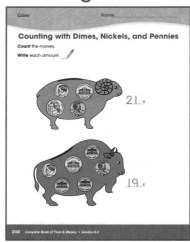

Coins   Name

Counting with Dimes, Nickels, and Pennies

Count the money.

Write each amount.

21¢

19¢

240   Complete Book of Time & Money • Grades K-3

Page 241

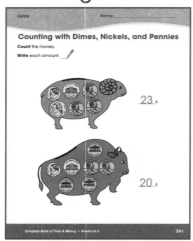

Coins   Name

Counting with Dimes, Nickels, and Pennies

Count the money.

Write each amount.

23¢

20¢

Complete Book of Time & Money • Grades K-3   241

Page 242

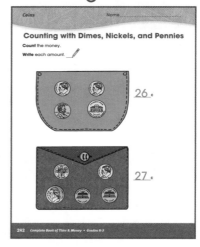

Coins   Name

Counting with Dimes, Nickels, and Pennies

Count the money.

Write each amount.

26¢

27¢

242   Complete Book of Time & Money • Grades K-3

Page 243

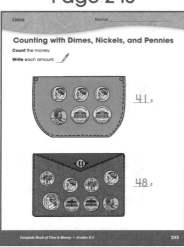

Coins   Name

Counting with Dimes, Nickels, and Pennies

Count the money.

Write each amount.

41¢

48¢

Complete Book of Time & Money • Grades K-3   243

Page 244

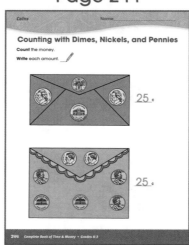

Coins   Name

Counting with Dimes, Nickels, and Pennies

Count the money.

Write each amount.

25¢

25¢

244   Complete Book of Time & Money • Grades K-3

Page 245

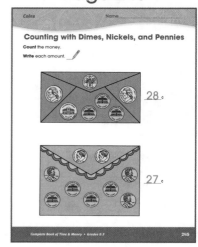

Coins   Name

Counting with Dimes, Nickels, and Pennies

Count the money.

Write each amount.

28¢

27¢

Complete Book of Time & Money • Grades K-3   245

Page 246

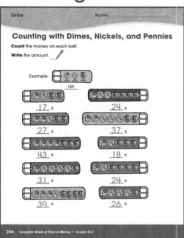

Page 247

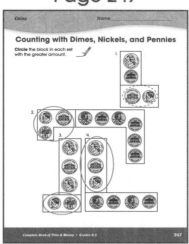

Page 248

Page 249

Page 250

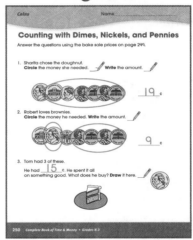

Page 251

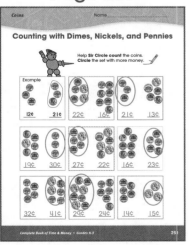

Page 252

Page 253

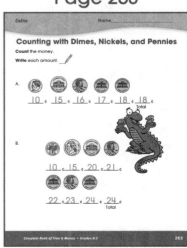

Page 254

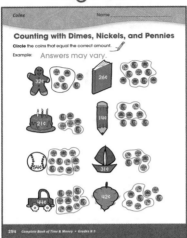

Page 255

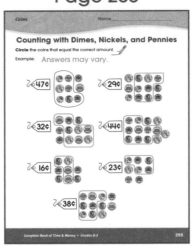

Page 256

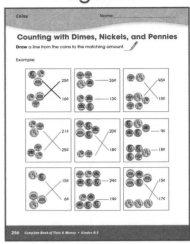

Page 257

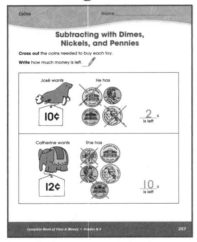

Page 258

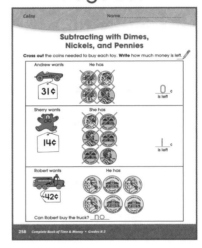

Page 259

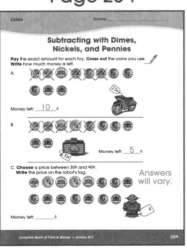

Page 260

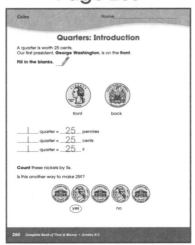

Page 261

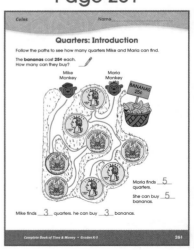

Answer Key

Page 262

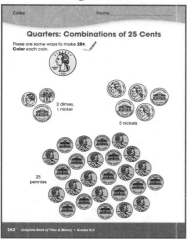

Page 263

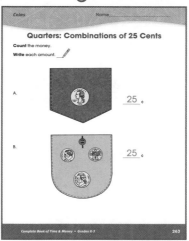

Page 264

Page 265

Page 266

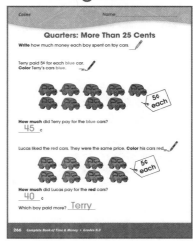

Page 267

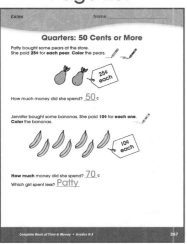

Page 268

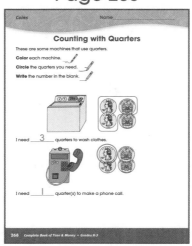

Page 269

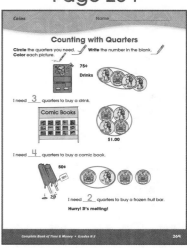

Page 270

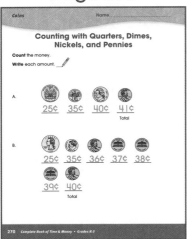

Coins   Name_____

Counting with Quarters, Dimes, Nickels, and Pennies

Count the money.

Write each amount.

A.   25¢   35¢   40¢   41¢
                              Total

B.   25¢   35¢   36¢   37¢   38¢

      39¢   40¢
            Total

270   Complete Book of Time & Money • Grades K-3

Page 271

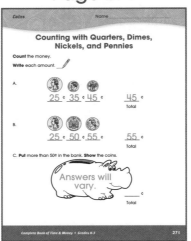

Coins   Name_____

Counting with Quarters, Dimes, Nickels, and Pennies

Count the money.

Write each amount.

A.   25¢   35¢   45¢   45 ¢
                            Total

B.   25¢   50¢   55¢   55 ¢
                            Total

C. **Put** more than 50¢ in the bank. **Show** the coins.

Answers will vary.

____ ¢
Total

Complete Book of Time & Money • Grades K-3   271

Page 272

Coins   Name_____

Counting with Quarters, Dimes, Nickels, and Pennies

Count the money. **Write** each amount.

A.   25 ¢ 35 ¢ 40 ¢ 41 ¢ 42 ¢ 42 ¢
                                      Total

B.   25 ¢ 35 ¢ 45 ¢ 50 ¢ 55 ¢ 56 ¢

      57 ¢ 58 ¢ 58 ¢
                  Total

I'm counting my money. 25¢, 35¢, 45¢, 55¢, 60¢, 65¢, 66¢, 67¢.

C. **Solve** this puzzle. What coins does Lizard have?

25¢ 10¢ 10¢ 10¢
5¢   5¢   1¢   1¢

272   Complete Book of Time & Money • Grades K-3

Page 273

Coins   Name_____

Counting with Quarters, Dimes, Nickels, and Pennies

Count the money.

Write each amount.

A.   36 ¢

B.   31 ¢

Complete Book of Time & Money • Grades K-3   273

Page 274

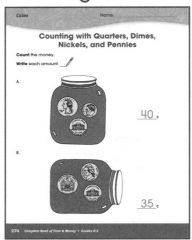

Coins   Name_____

Counting with Quarters, Dimes, Nickels, and Pennies

Count the money.

Write each amount.

A.   40 ¢

B.   35 ¢

274   Complete Book of Time & Money • Grades K-3

Page 275

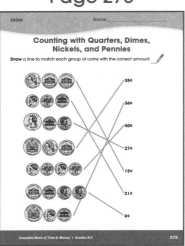

Coins   Name_____

Counting with Quarters, Dimes, Nickels, and Pennies

Draw a line to match each group of coins with the correct amount.

35¢
36¢
40¢
27¢
15¢
21¢
8¢

Complete Book of Time & Money • Grades K-3   275

Page 276

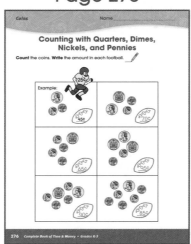

Coins   Name_____

Counting with Quarters, Dimes, Nickels, and Pennies

Count the coins. **Write** the amount in each football.

Example: 45¢   70¢

            65¢   95¢

            50¢   85¢

276   Complete Book of Time & Money • Grades K-3

Page 277

Coins   Name_____

Counting with Quarters, Dimes, Nickels, and Pennies

Count the coins. **Write** each amount.
Do you have enough money to buy each toy?

	You have...		yes or no
Example:	58¢	51¢	no
	47¢	57¢	yes
	75¢	76¢	yes
	43¢	51¢	yes
	98¢	80¢	no
	32¢	25¢	no
	26¢	29¢	yes
	45¢	35¢	no

Complete Book of Time & Money • Grades K-3   277

Page 278

Page 279

Page 280

Page 281

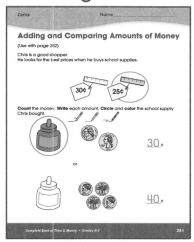

Page 282

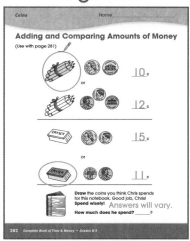

Page 283

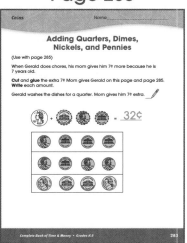

Page 285

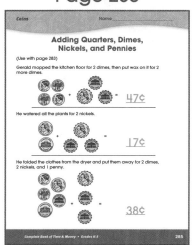

Page 286

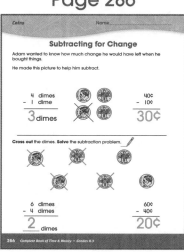

Answer Key

Page 287

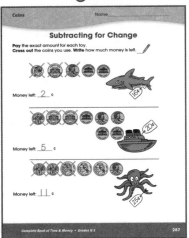

Coins   Name_____

Subtracting for Change

Pay the exact amount for each toy.
Cross out the coins you use. **Write** how much money is left.

Money left: _2_ ¢

Money left: _5_ ¢

Money left: _11_ ¢

Page 288

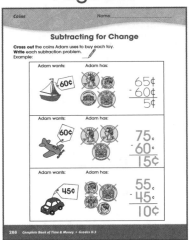

Coins   Name_____

Subtracting for Change

Cross out the coins Adam uses to buy each toy.
Write each subtraction problem.
Example:

Adam wants:	Adam has:	
60¢		65¢ - 60¢ = 5¢
60¢		75¢ - 60¢ = 15¢
45¢		55¢ - 45¢ = 10¢

Page 289

Coins   Name_____

Subtracting from 50 Cents

Maria went to the store to buy a birthday gift for her best friend.

Maria took 50¢ to the store.

Circle each thing Maria can buy.

16¢   29¢

32¢

65¢   36¢

Page 290

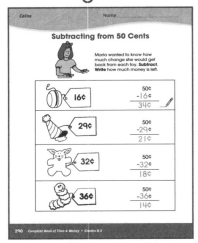

Coins   Name_____

Subtracting from 50 Cents

Maria wanted to know how much change she would get back from each toy. **Subtract.**
Write how much money is left.

16¢	50¢ -16¢	34¢
29¢	50¢ -29¢	21¢
32¢	50¢ -32¢	18¢
36¢	50¢ -36¢	14¢

Page 291

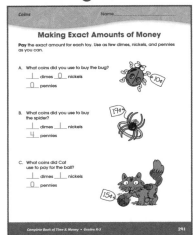

Coins   Name_____

Making Exact Amounts of Money

Pay the exact amount for each toy. Use as few dimes, nickels, and pennies as you can.

A. What coins did you use to buy the bug?
_1_ dimes _0_ nickels
_0_ pennies   10¢

B. What coins did you use to buy the spider?
_1_ dimes _1_ nickels
_4_ pennies   19¢

C. What coins did Cat use to pay for the ball?
_1_ dimes _1_ nickels
_0_ pennies   15¢

Page 292

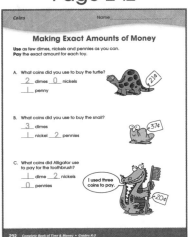

Coins   Name_____

Making Exact Amounts of Money

Use as few dimes, nickels and pennies as you can.
Pay the exact amount for each toy.

A. What coins did you use to buy the turtle?
_2_ dimes _0_ nickels
_1_ penny   21¢

B. What coins did you use to buy the snail?
_3_ dimes
_1_ nickel _2_ pennies   37¢

C. What coins did Alligator use to pay for the toothbrush?
_1_ dime _2_ nickels
_0_ pennies

I used three coins to pay.   20¢

Page 293

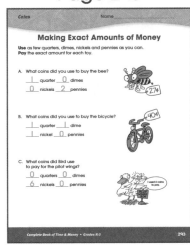

Coins   Name_____

Making Exact Amounts of Money

Use as few quarters, dimes, nickels and pennies as you can.
Pay the exact amount for each toy.

A. What coins did you use to buy the bee?
_1_ quarter _0_ dimes
_0_ nickels _2_ pennies   27¢

B. What coins did you use to buy the bicycle?
_1_ quarter _1_ dime
_1_ nickel _0_ pennies   40¢

C. What coins did Bird use to pay for the pilot wings?
_0_ quarters _0_ dimes
_6_ nickels _0_ pennies

I used 6 coins to pay.

Page 294

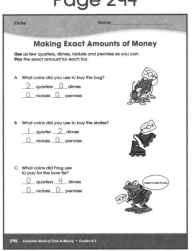

Coins   Name_____

Making Exact Amounts of Money

Use as few quarters, dimes, nickels and pennies as you can.
Pay the exact amount for each toy.

A. What coins did you use to buy the bug?
_2_ quarters _0_ dimes
_0_ nickels _0_ pennies   50¢

B. What coins did you use to buy the skates?
_1_ quarter _2_ dimes
_0_ nickels _0_ pennies   45¢

C. What coins did Frog use to pay for the bow tie?
_0_ quarters _4_ dimes
_0_ nickels _0_ pennies

I used 4 coins to pay.   40¢

Answer Key

Page 295

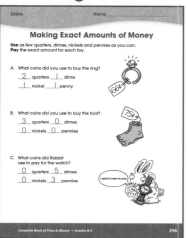

Coins — Name

Making Exact Amounts of Money

Use as few quarters, dimes, nickels and pennies as you can.
Pay the exact amount for each toy.

A. What coins did you use to buy the ring?
_2_ quarters _1_ dime
_1_ nickel _1_ penny

B. What coins did you use to buy the foot?
_3_ quarters _0_ dimes
_0_ nickels _0_ pennies

C. What coins did Rabbit use to pay for the watch?
_0_ quarters _5_ dimes
_0_ nickels _3_ pennies

Page 296

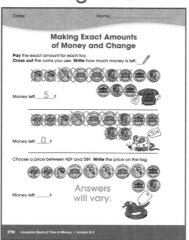

Coins — Name

Making Exact Amounts of Money and Change

Pay the exact amount for each toy.
Cross out the coins you use. **Write** how much money is left.

Money left: _5_ ¢

Money left: _0_ ¢

Choose a price between 42¢ and 58¢. **Write** the price on the tag.

Money left: _____ ¢

Answers will vary.

Page 297

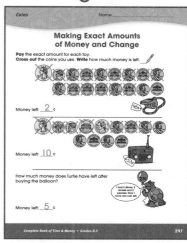

Coins — Name

Making Exact Amounts of Money and Change

Pay the exact amount for each toy.
Cross out the coins you use. **Write** how much money is left.

Money left: _2_ ¢

Money left: _10_ ¢

How much money does Turtle have left after buying the balloon?

Money left: _5_ ¢

Page 298

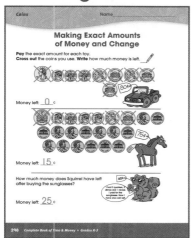

Coins — Name

Making Exact Amounts of Money and Change

Pay the exact amount for each toy.
Cross out the coins you use. **Write** how much money is left.

Money left: _0_ ¢

Money left: _15_ ¢

How much money does Squirrel have left after buying the sunglasses?

Money left: _25_ ¢

Page 299

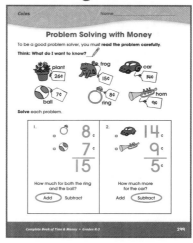

Coins — Name

Problem Solving with Money

To be a good problem solver, you must **read the problem carefully.**

Think: What do I want to know?

plant 26¢   frog 15¢   car 14¢
ball 7¢   ring 8¢   horn 9¢

Solve each problem.

1.
$$\begin{array}{r} 8¢ \\ 7 \\ \hline 15 \end{array}$$
How much for both the ring and the ball?
(Add)   Subtract

2.
$$\begin{array}{r} 14¢ \\ 9 \\ \hline 5¢ \end{array}$$
How much more for the car?
Add   (Subtract)

Page 300

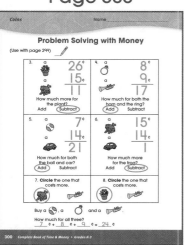

Coins — Name

Problem Solving with Money

(Use with page 299)

3.
$$\begin{array}{r} 26¢ \\ 15 \\ \hline 11 \end{array}$$
How much more for the plant?
Add   (Subtract)

4.
$$\begin{array}{r} 8¢ \\ 9 \\ \hline 17 \end{array}$$
How much for both the horn and the ring?
(Add)   Subtract

5.
$$\begin{array}{r} 7 \\ 14¢ \\ \hline 21 \end{array}$$
How much for both the ball and car?
(Add)   Subtract

6.
$$\begin{array}{r} 15¢ \\ 14 \\ \hline 1 \end{array}$$
How much more for the frog?
Add   (Subtract)

7. **Circle** the one that costs more.

8. **Circle** the one that costs more.

Buy a ☐, a ○ and a ▽.
How much for all three?
_7_ ¢ + _8_ ¢ + _9_ = _24_ ¢

Page 301

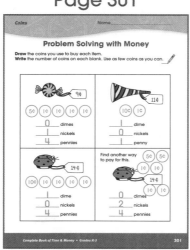

Coins — Name

Problem Solving with Money

Draw the coins you use to buy each item.
Write the number of coins on each blank. Use as few coins as you can.

9¢   5¢ 1¢ 1¢ 1¢ 1¢
_0_ dimes
_1_ nickels
_4_ pennies

11¢   10¢ 1¢
_1_ dime
_0_ nickels
_1_ penny

14¢   10¢ 1¢ 1¢ 1¢ 1¢
_1_ dime
_0_ nickels
_4_ pennies

Find another way to pay for this.   5¢ 5¢ 1¢ 1¢ 14¢
_0_ dimes
_2_ nickels
_4_ pennies

Page 302

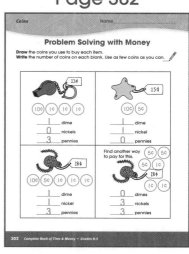

Coins — Name

Problem Solving with Money

Draw the coins you use to buy each item.
Write the number of coins on each blank. Use as few coins as you can.

13¢   10¢ 1¢ 1¢ 1¢
_1_ dime
_0_ nickels
_3_ pennies

15¢   10¢ 5¢
_1_ dime
_1_ nickel
_0_ pennies

18¢   10¢ 5¢ 1¢ 1¢ 1¢
_1_ dime
_1_ nickel
_3_ pennies

Find another way to pay for this.   5¢ 5¢ 5¢ 1¢ 1¢ 1¢ 18¢
_0_ dimes
_3_ nickels
_3_ pennies

Page 303

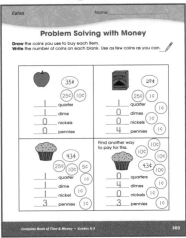

Page 304

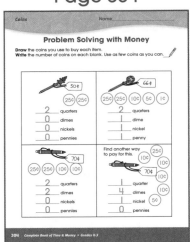

Page 305

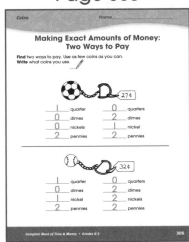

Page 306

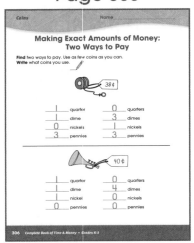

Page 307

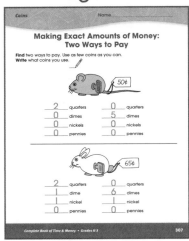

Page 308

Page 309

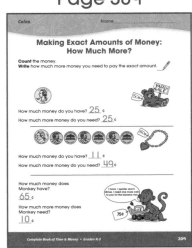

Page 310

Answer Key

Page 311

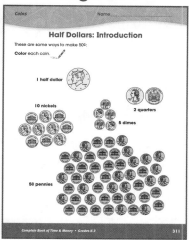

Page 312

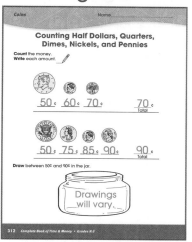

Page 313

Page 314

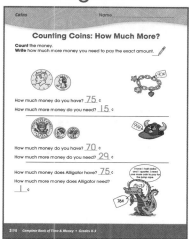

Page 315

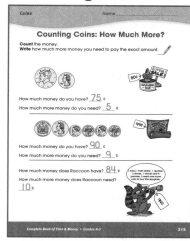

Page 316

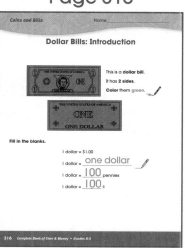

Page 317

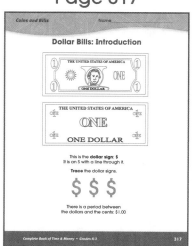

Page 319

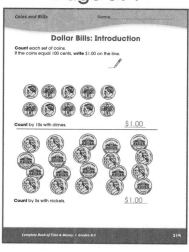

Answer Key

Page 320

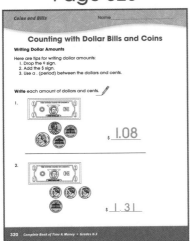

Page 321

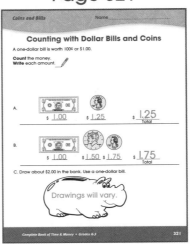

Page 322

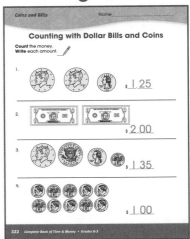

Page 323

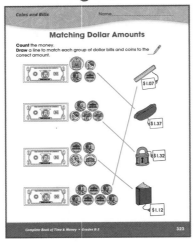

Page 324

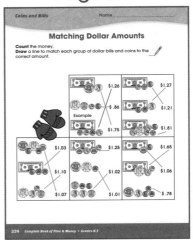

Page 325

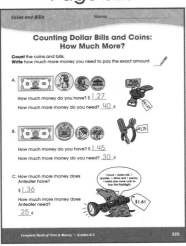

Page 326

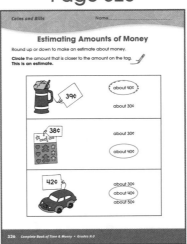

Page 327

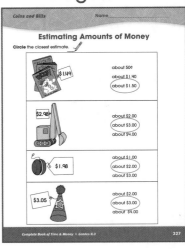

Answer Key

Page 328

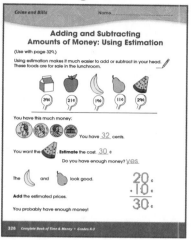

Page 329

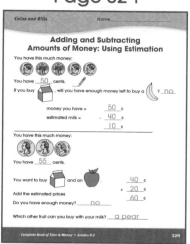

Page 330

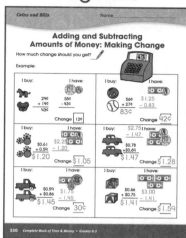

Page 331

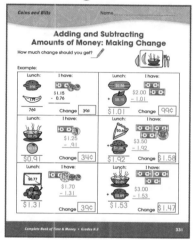

Page 332

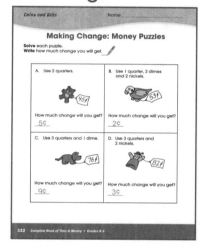

Page 333

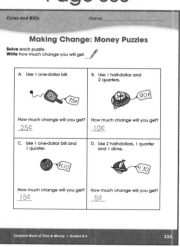

Page 334

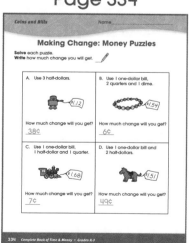

Page 335

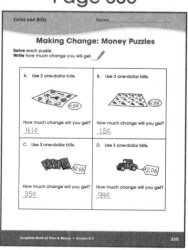

Answer Key

Page 336

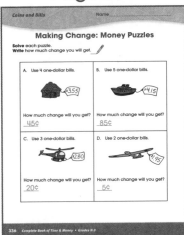

Coins and Bills   Name_____

Making Change: Money Puzzles

Solve each puzzle.
Write how much change you will get.

A. Use 4 one-dollar bills.
$3.55
How much change will you get?
45¢

B. Use 5 one-dollar bills.
$4.15
How much change will you get?
85¢

C. Use 3 one-dollar bills.
$2.80
How much change will you get?
20¢

D. Use 2 one-dollar bills.
$1.95
How much change will you get?
5¢

336   Complete Book of Time & Money • Grades K-3

Page 337

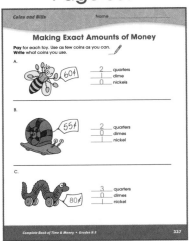

Coins and Bills   Name_____

Making Exact Amounts of Money

Pay for each toy. Use as few coins as you can.
Write what coins you use.

A. 60¢
2 quarters
1 dime
0 nickels

B. 55¢
2 quarters
0 dimes
1 nickel

C. 80¢
3 quarters
0 dimes
1 nickel

337

Page 338

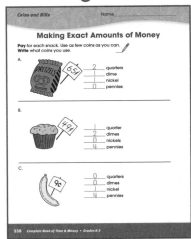

Coins and Bills   Name_____

Making Exact Amounts of Money

Pay for each snack. Use as few coins as you can.
Write what coins you use.

A. 65¢
2 quarters
1 dime
1 nickel
0 pennies

B. 49¢
1 quarter
2 dimes
0 nickels
4 pennies

C. 9¢
0 quarters
0 dimes
1 nickel
4 pennies

338   Complete Book of Time & Money • Grades K-3

Page 339

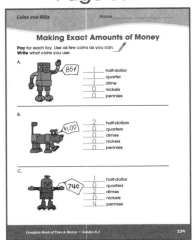

Coins and Bills   Name_____

Making Exact Amounts of Money

Pay for each toy. Use as few coins as you can.
Write what coins you use.

A. 85¢
1 half-dollar
1 quarter
1 dime
0 nickels
0 pennies

B. $1.00
2 half-dollars
0 quarters
0 dimes
0 nickels
0 pennies

C. 74¢
1 half-dollar
0 quarters
2 dimes
0 nickels
4 pennies

Complete Book of Time & Money • Grades K-3   339

Page 340

Coins and Bills   Name_____

Making Exact Amounts of Money

Pay for each toy. Use as few coins as you can.
Write what coins you use.

A. $1.50
3 half-dollars
0 quarters
0 dimes
0 nickels
0 pennies

B. $1.35
2 half-dollars
1 quarter
1 dime
0 nickels
0 pennies

C. 98¢
1 half-dollar
1 quarter
2 dimes
0 nickels
3 pennies

340   Complete Book of Time & Money • Grades K-3

Page 341

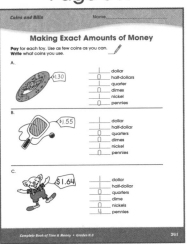

Coins and Bills   Name_____

Making Exact Amounts of Money

Pay for each toy. Use as few coins as you can.
Write what coins you use.

A. $1.30
1 dollar
0 half-dollars
1 quarter
0 dimes
1 nickel
0 pennies

B. $1.55
1 dollar
1 half-dollar
0 quarters
0 dimes
1 nickel
0 pennies

C. $1.64
1 dollar
1 half-dollar
0 quarters
1 dime
0 nickels
4 pennies

Complete Book of Time & Money • Grades K-3   341

Page 342

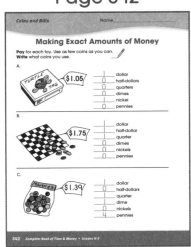

Coins and Bills   Name_____

Making Exact Amounts of Money

Pay for each toy. Use as few coins as you can.
Write what coins you use.

A. $1.05
1 dollar
0 half-dollar
0 quarters
0 dimes
1 nickel
0 pennies

B. $1.75
1 dollar
1 half-dollar
1 quarter
0 dimes
0 nickels
0 pennies

C. $1.39
1 dollar
0 half-dollars
1 quarter
1 dime
0 nickels
4 pennies

342   Complete Book of Time & Money • Grades K-3

Page 343

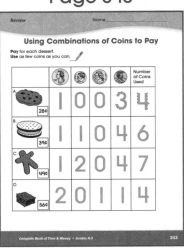

Review   Name_____

Using Combinations of Coins to Pay

Pay for each dessert.
Use as few coins as you can.

					Number of Coins Used
A. 28¢	1	0	0	3	4
B. 39¢	1	1	0	4	6
C. 49¢	1	2	0	4	7
D. 56¢	2	0	1	1	4

Complete Book of Time & Money • Grades K-3   343

Page 344

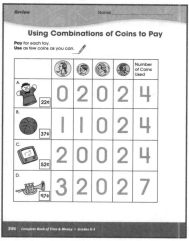

Review   Name_____

Using Combinations of Coins to Pay

Pay for each toy.
Use as few coins as you can.

					Number of Coins Used
A. 22¢	0	2	0	2	4
B. 37¢	1	1	0	2	4
C. 52¢	2	0	0	2	4
D. 97¢	3	2	0	2	7

Page 345

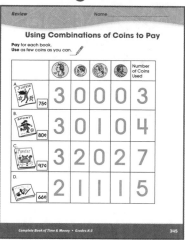

Review   Name_____

Using Combinations of Coins to Pay

Pay for each book.
Use as few coins as you can.

					Number of Coins Used
A. 75¢	3	0	0	0	3
B. 80¢	3	0	1	0	4
C. 97¢	3	2	0	2	7
D. 66¢	2	1	1	1	5

Page 346

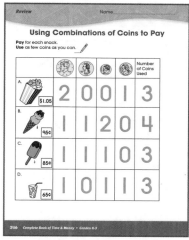

Review   Name_____

Using Combinations of Coins to Pay

Pay for each snack.
Use as few coins as you can.

					Number of Coins Used
A. $1.05	2	0	0	1	3
B. 95¢	1	1	2	0	4
C. 85¢	1	1	1	0	3
D. 65¢	1	0	1	1	3

Page 347

Review   Name_____

Using Combinations of Coins to Pay

Pay for each mask.
Use as few coins and bills as you can.

					Number of Coins Used
A. $1.75	1	3	0	0	4
B. $1.95	1	3	2	0	6
C. $2.50	2	2	0	0	4
D. $3.15	3	0	1	1	5

Page 348

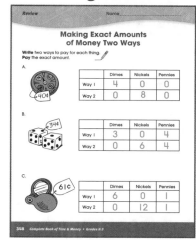

Review   Name_____

Making Exact Amounts of Money Two Ways

Write two ways to pay for each thing.
Pay the exact amount.

A. 40¢

	Dimes	Nickels	Pennies
Way 1	4	0	0
Way 2	0	8	0

B. 34¢

	Dimes	Nickels	Pennies
Way 1	3	0	4
Way 2	0	6	4

C. 61¢

	Dimes	Nickels	Pennies
Way 1	6	0	1
Way 2	0	12	1

Page 349

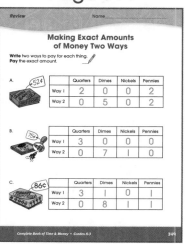

Review   Name_____

Making Exact Amounts of Money Two Ways

Write two ways to pay for each thing.
Pay the exact amount.

A. 52¢

	Quarters	Dimes	Nickels	Pennies
Way 1	2	0	0	2
Way 2	0	5	0	2

B. 75¢

	Quarters	Dimes	Nickels	Pennies
Way 1	3	0	0	0
Way 2	0	7	1	0

C. 86¢

	Quarters	Dimes	Nickels	Pennies
Way 1	3	1	0	1
Way 2	0	8	1	1

Page 350

Review   Name_____

Making Exact Amounts of Money Two Ways

Write two ways to pay for each thing.
Pay the exact amount.

A. $1.25

	Half Dollars	Quarters	Dimes	Nickels	Pennies
Way 1	2	1	0	0	0
Way 2	0	5	0	0	0

B. $1.50

	Half Dollars	Quarters	Dimes	Nickels	Pennies
Way 1	3	0	0	0	0
Way 2	0	6	0	0	0

C. $1.17

	Half Dollars	Quarters	Dimes	Nickels	Pennies
Way 1	2	0	1	1	2
Way 2	0	4	0	3	2

Page 351

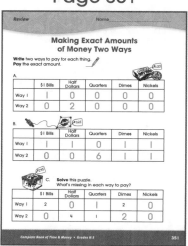

Review   Name_____

Making Exact Amounts of Money Two Ways

Write two ways to pay for each thing.
Pay the exact amount.

A. $1.00

	$1 Bills	Half Dollars	Quarters	Dimes	Nickels
Way 1	1	0	0	0	0
Way 2	0	2	0	0	0

B. $1.65

	$1 Bills	Half Dollars	Quarters	Dimes	Nickels
Way 1	1	1	0	1	1
Way 2	0	0	6	1	1

C. $1.70 **Solve** this puzzle.
What's missing in each way to pay?

	$1 Bills	Half Dollars	Quarters	Dimes	Nickels
Way 1	2	0	1	2	0
Way 2	0	4	1	2	0

Page 352

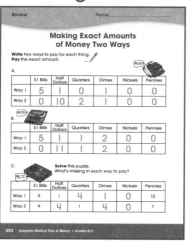

Making Exact Amounts of Money Two Ways

Write two ways to pay for each thing.
Pay the exact amount.

A.

	$1 Bills	Half Dollars	Quarters	Dimes	Nickels	Pennies
Way 1	5	1	0	1	0	0
Way 2	0	10	2	1	0	0

B.

	$1 Bills	Half Dollars	Quarters	Dimes	Nickels	Pennies
Way 1	5	1	1	2	0	0
Way 2	0	11	1	2	0	0

C. **Solve** this puzzle. What's missing in each way to pay?

	$1 Bills	Half Dollars	Quarters	Dimes	Nickels	Pennies
Way 1	5	1	4	1	0	12
Way 2	4	4	4	4	0	7

Page 353

Estimating Amounts of Money

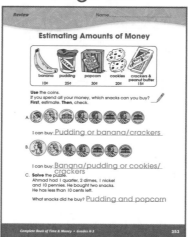

banana 10¢   pudding 25¢   popcorn 30¢   cookies 20¢   crackers & peanut butter 15¢

Use the coins.
If you spend all your money, which snacks can you buy?
First, estimate. **Then**, check.

A. I can buy: Pudding or banana/crackers

B. I can buy: Banana/pudding or cookies/crackers

C. **Solve** the puzzle.
Ahmad had 1 quarter, 2 dimes, 1 nickel and 10 pennies. He bought two snacks. He has less than 10 cents left.

What snacks did he buy? Pudding and popcorn

Page 354

Estimating Amounts of Money

25¢   65¢   50¢   55¢   70¢   35¢

Use the coins.
If you spend all your money, which pet treats can you buy? **First**, estimate. **Then**, check.

A. I can buy: Bird seed and turtle delight

B. I can buy: Kitty treats and dog cookies

C. **Solve** the puzzle.
Ismelda had 3 quarters. She bought a pet treat. She has 2 quarters left.

What treat did she buy? Beef munchies

Page 355

Estimating Amounts of Money

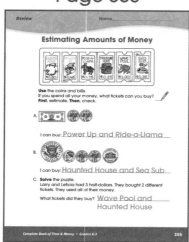

$0.50 $0.45 $0.75 $0.25 $1.00 $0.35

Use the coins and bills
If you spend all your money, what tickets can you buy?
First, estimate. **Then**, check.

A. I can buy: Power Up and Ride-a-Llama

B. I can buy: Haunted House and Sea Sub

C. **Solve** the puzzle.
Larry and Leticia had 3 half-dollars. They bought 2 different tickets. They used all of their money.

What tickets did they buy? Wave Pool and Haunted House

Page 356

Estimating Amounts of Money

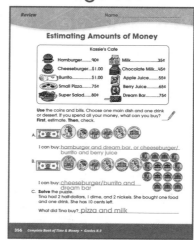

Kassie's Cafe

Hamburger........90¢	Milk.....................35¢
Cheeseburger...$1.00	Chocolate Milk...45¢
Burrito...............$1.00	Apple Juice..........55¢
Small Pizza......75¢	Berry Juice..........65¢
Super Salad......80¢	Dream Bar..........75¢

Use the coins and bills. Choose one main dish and one drink or dessert. If you spend all your money, what can you buy?
First, estimate. **Then**, check.

A. I can buy: hamburger and dream bar, or cheeseburger/burrito and berry juice

B. I can buy: cheeseburger/burrito and dream bar

C. **Solve** the puzzle.
Tina had 2 half-dollars, 1 dime, and 2 nickels. She bought one food and one drink. She has 10 cents left.

What did Tina buy? pizza and milk

Page 357

Estimating Amounts of Money

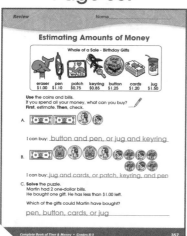

Whale of a Sale - Birthday Gifts

eraser $1.00   pen $1.10   patch $0.75   keyring $0.85   button $1.25   cards $1.20   jug $1.50

Use the coins and bills.
If you spend all your money, what can you buy?
First, estimate. **Then**, check.

A. I can buy: button and pen, or jug and keyring

B. I can buy: jug and cards, or patch, keyring, and pen

C. **Solve** the puzzle.
Martin had 2 one-dollar bills. He bought one gift. He has less than $1.00 left.

Which of the gifts could Martin have bought?

pen, button, cards, or jug

Page 358

Making Change

Pay the exact amount.
Write how much change you will get back.

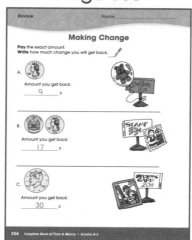

A. Amount you get back: 9 ¢

B. Amount you get back: 17 ¢

C. Amount you get back: 30 ¢

Page 359

Making Change

Pay the exact amount.
Write how much change you will get back.

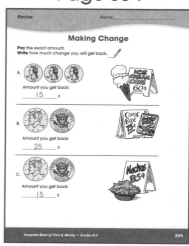

A. Amount you get back: 15 ¢

B. Amount you get back: 25 ¢

C. Amount you get back: 15 ¢

Answer Key

Page 360

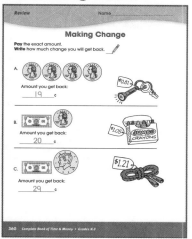

Review   Name _____

Making Change

Pay the exact amount.
Write how much change you will get back.

A. Amount you get back:
19 ¢

B. Amount you get back:
20 ¢

C. Amount you get back:
29 ¢

360   Complete Book of Time & Money • Grades K-3

Page 361

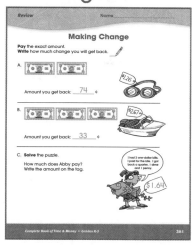

Review   Name _____

Making Change

Pay the exact amount.
Write how much change you will get back.

A. Amount you get back: 74 ¢

B. Amount you get back: 33 ¢

C. **Solve** the puzzle.
How much does Abby pay?
Write the amount on the tag.
$1.64

Complete Book of Time & Money • Grades K-3   361

Page 362

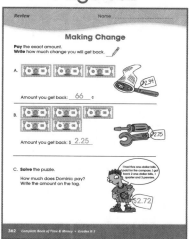

Review   Name _____

Making Change

Pay the exact amount.
Write how much change you will get back.

A. Amount you get back: 66 ¢

B. Amount you get back: $ 2.25

C. **Solve** the puzzle.
How much does Dominic pay?
Write the amount on the tag.
$2.72

362   Complete Book of Time & Money • Grades K-3

Page 363

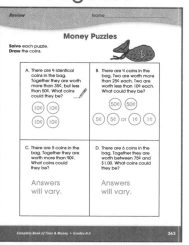

Review   Name _____

Money Puzzles

Solve each puzzle.
Draw the coins.

A. There are 4 identical coins in the bag. Together they are worth more than 35¢, but less than 50¢. What coins could they be?
10¢ 10¢ 10¢ 10¢

B. There are 4 coins in the bag. Two are worth more than 25¢ each. Two are worth less than 10¢ each. What could they be?
50¢ 50¢ 5¢ 5¢ or 50¢ 50¢ 1¢ 1¢

C. There are 5 coins in the bag. Together they are worth more than 90¢. What coins could they be?
Answers will vary.

D. There are 6 coins in the bag. Together they are worth between 75¢ and $1.00. What coins could they be?
Answers will vary.

Complete Book of Time & Money • Grades K-3   363

Page 364

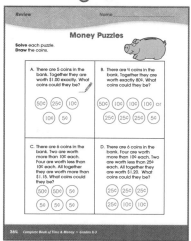

Review   Name _____

Money Puzzles

Solve each puzzle.
Draw the coins.

A. There are 5 coins in the bank. Together they are worth $1.00 exactly. What coins could they be?
50¢ 25¢ 10¢ 10¢ 5¢

B. There are 4 coins in the bank. Together they are worth exactly 80¢. What coins could they be?
50¢ 10¢ 10¢ 10¢ or 25¢ 25¢ 25¢ 5¢

C. There are 6 coins in the bank. Two are worth more than 10¢ each. Four are worth less than 10¢ each. All together they are worth more than $1.15. What coins could they be?
50¢ 50¢ 5¢ 5¢ 5¢ 5¢

D. There are 6 coins in the bank. Four are worth more than 10¢ each. Two are worth less than 25¢ each. All together they are worth $1.20. What coins could they be?
25¢ 25¢ 25¢ 25¢ 10¢ 10¢

364   Complete Book of Time & Money • Grades K-3

Page 365

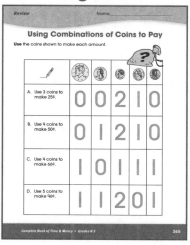

Review   Name _____

Using Combinations of Coins to Pay

Use the coins shown to make each amount.

A. Use 3 coins to make 25¢.	0	0	2	1	0
B. Use 4 coins to make 50¢.	0	1	2	1	0
C. Use 4 coins to make 66¢.	1	0	1	1	1
D. Use 5 coins to make 96¢.	1	1	2	0	1

Complete Book of Time & Money • Grades K-3   365

Page 366

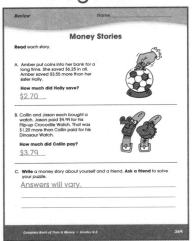

Review   Name_____

Using Combinations of Coins to Pay

Use the coins shown to make each amount.

A. Use 3 coins to make 60¢. What coins did you use?	0	2	1	0
B. What other way can you do it?	1	0	0	2
C. Use 4 coins to make 40¢. What coins did you use?	0	0	4	0
D. What other way can you do it?	0	1	0	3
E. Use 4 coins to make 80¢. What coins did you use?	0	3	0	1
F. What other way can you do it?	1	0	3	0

366   Complete Book of Time & Money • Grades K-3

Page 367

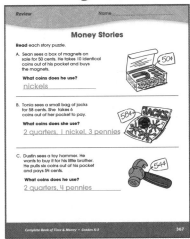

Review   Name_____

Money Stories

Read each story puzzle.

A. Sean sees a box of magnets on sale for 50 cents. He takes 10 identical coins out of his pocket and buys the magnets.

What coins does he use?

nickels

B. Tonia sees a small bag of jacks for 58 cents. She takes 6 coins out of her pocket to pay.

What coins does she use?

2 quarters, 1 nickel, 3 pennies

C. Dustin sees a toy hammer. He wants to buy it for his little brother. He pulls six coins out of his pocket and pays 54 cents.

What coins does he use?

2 quarters, 4 pennies

Complete Book of Time & Money • Grades K-3   367

Page 368

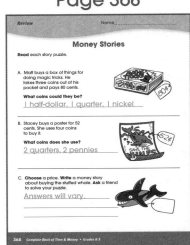

Review   Name_____

Money Stories

Read each story puzzle.

A. Matt buys a box of things for doing magic tricks. He takes three coins out of his pocket and pays 80 cents.

What coins could they be?

1 half-dollar, 1 quarter, 1 nickel

B. Stacey buys a poster for 52 cents. She uses four coins to buy it.

What coins does she use?

2 quarters, 2 pennies

C. **Choose** a price. **Write** a money story about buying the stuffed whale. **Ask** a friend to solve your puzzle.

Answers will vary.

368   Complete Book of Time & Money • Grades K-3

Page 369

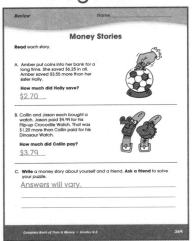

Review   Name_____

Money Stories

Read each story.

A. Amber put coins into her bank for a long time. She saved $6.25 in all. Amber saved $3.55 more than her sister Holly.

How much did Holly save?

$2.70

B. Collin and Jason each bought a watch. Jason paid $4.99 for his Flip-up Crocodile Watch. That was $1.20 more than Collin paid for his Dinosaur Watch.

How much did Collin pay?

$3.79

C. **Write** a money story about yourself and a friend. **Ask** a friend to solve your puzzle.

Answers will vary.

Complete Book of Time & Money • Grades K-3   369

Page 370

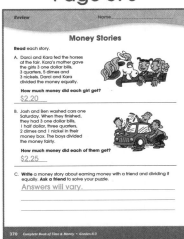

Review   Name_____

Money Stories

Read each story.

A. Darci and Kara fed the horses at the fair. Kara's mother gave the girls 3 one dollar bills, 3 quarters, 5 dimes and 3 nickels. Darci and Kara divided the money equally.

How much money did each girl get?

$2.20

B. Josh and Ben washed cars one Saturday. When they finished, they had 3 one dollar bills, 1 half dollar, three quarters, 2 dimes and 1 nickel in their money box. The boys divided the money fairly.

How much money did each of them get?

$2.25

C. **Write** a money story about earning money with a friend and dividing it equally. **Ask** a friend to solve your puzzle.

Answers will vary.

370   Complete Book of Time & Money • Grades K-3

Page 371

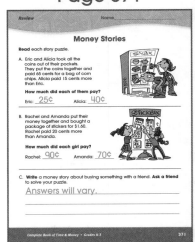

Review   Name_____

Money Stories

Read each story puzzle.

A. Eric and Alicia took all the coins out of their pockets. They put the coins together and paid 65 cents for a bag of corn chips. Alicia paid 15 cents more than Eric.

How much did each of them pay?

Eric: 25¢   Alicia: 40¢

B. Rachel and Amanda put their money together and bought a package of stickers for $1.60. Rachel paid 20 cents more than Amanda.

How much did each girl pay?

Rachel: 90¢   Amanda: 70¢

C. **Write** a money story about buying something with a friend. **Ask** a friend to solve your puzzle.

Answers will vary.

Complete Book of Time & Money • Grades K-3   371